The $500,000 Vending Machine Equation: How to Start a Vending Machine Small Business and Bring to Scale in 1 Year

Master Branding with Social Media, Innovation Investing & The Product Mix Data Potion

David Whitehead

Silk Publishing

Contents

A Frustrating Spark

Opportunities don't happen. You create them.

— Chris Grosser

It was a typical workday, the kind where every minute seemed to stretch on endlessly. The clock ticked slower than usual, and my stomach growled in protest as lunchtime approached. Eager for a quick snack to tide me over, I made my way to the break room, where the vending machine stood like a beacon of hope. I had a craving for a chocolate bar, something to give me that extra bit of energy to push through the rest of the afternoon.

With a few crumpled dollar bills in hand, I approached the machine, feeling confident that my snack was just moments away. I inserted the money, pressed the button for my desired treat, and waited. But instead of the familiar whir of the machine delivering my selection, I was met with an unsettling silence. The machine hummed softly, the display flickered, and then— nothing. My chocolate bar remained stubbornly in place, taunting me from behind the glass.

I pressed the button again, a bit more forcefully this time, hoping it would make a difference. Still nothing. I tried another selection, thinking perhaps it was just a fluke with that particular slot. Again, my efforts were in vain. Frustration began to set in. I had just lost my money to a malfunctioning machine, and my craving for that chocolate bar was now overshadowed by a growing annoyance.

As I stood there, contemplating my next move, I couldn't help but notice the expressions of others who approached the machine after me. They, too, encountered the same problem, shaking their heads in disappointment and walking away empty-handed. It was then that a thought crossed my mind: why do vending machines fail so often? And more importantly, what could be done to fix this recurring issue?

This experience, though minor in the grand scheme of things, planted a seed in my mind. I began to think about all the times I had encountered similar problems with vending machines—coins getting stuck, items not dispensing, or machines simply being out of order. Each instance was a small inconvenience, but collectively, they painted a picture of an industry rife with reliability issues. Could there be a way to improve the vending machine experience, ensuring that customers always got what they paid for?

Driven by this question, I started researching the vending machine industry. I wanted to understand why these machines failed and what could be done to prevent such issues. I discovered that many common problems stemmed from outdated technology, poor maintenance, and subpar machine design. The more I learned, the more I realized there was a significant opportunity to create a better vending experience.

I decided to dive deeper. I looked into reliable vending machine suppliers, analyzing the different types of machines available on the market. I wanted machines that were not only robust and efficient but also equipped with the latest technology. My goal was to offer a variety of products, from snacks and drinks to healthier options, all while ensuring that the machines worked flawlessly.

Understanding the costs involved was the next step. I broke down the initial investment needed to purchase the machines, stock them with inventory, and maintain them regularly. I wanted to be prepared for any potential issues, so I factored in costs for repairs and routine maintenance. It was essential to have a clear financial plan to ensure that my business could run smoothly without unexpected disruptions.

Product selection was another critical area of focus. I wanted to offer something for everyone, catering to different tastes and dietary preferences. This meant conducting market research to understand what products were in demand and how to price them competitively. I also considered the importance of rotating products regularly to keep the offerings fresh and appealing.

But beyond the machines and products, I knew that customer experience would be key to my success. I envisioned a vending machine business that stood out for its reliability and customer satisfaction. To achieve this, I planned to implement rigorous maintenance schedules, ensuring that the machines were always clean, well-stocked, and in perfect working order. I also looked into integrating cashless payment options, making it easier and more convenient for customers to make purchases.

Social media emerged as a powerful tool in my strategy. By creating a strong online presence, I could engage with customers, gather feedback, and promote my vending locations. Social media platforms offered a way to build a community around my brand, sharing updates, new product offerings, and promotions to keep customers informed and excited.

As I pieced together my business plan, I realized that my initial frustration with a malfunctioning vending machine had transformed into a journey of entrepreneurship. That small moment of annoyance had sparked a determination to improve the vending machine industry, offering customers a reliable and enjoyable experience. My goal was not just to sell snacks but to create a brand synonymous with quality and dependability.

Chapter 1
The Foundation: Understanding the Variables

Vending machines are everywhere – in office buildings, schools, hospitals, and even at the corner of your street. They provide convenient access to snacks, beverages, and essential items 24/7. But behind every machine is a story of persistence, innovation, and a drive to meet customer needs efficiently and reliably.

When you decide to enter the vending machine business, you're stepping into an industry that balances low overhead with the potential for high recurring revenue. This business model offers significant advantages, including minimal staffing requirements and the flexibility to manage your operations on your terms. It's a venture that allows you to blend work and life seamlessly, giving you the freedom to pursue other interests or commitments while your machines work for you.

Your journey starts with a clear vision. What do you want to achieve? Perhaps you aim to promote healthy snacking options, provide quick and easy access to essential items, or simply generate a steady stream of passive income. Your vision will guide your decisions and shape your business strategy. By lever-aging the power of social media, you can align your personal motivations with your business goals, creating a brand that resonates with your target audience and builds a loyal customer base.

Launching Your Vending Machine Journey

The Vending Machine Advantage

Starting a business can be a daunting prospect, often associated with significant financial risk and time commitment. However, the vending machine industry presents a unique opportunity that stands out due to its low overhead, potential for recurring revenue, and the promise of a better work-life balance.

Firstly, let's talk about low overhead. Many traditional businesses require a substantial upfront investment. Think about the costs associated with renting a physical storefront, hiring employees, and maintaining day-to-day operations. These expenses can quickly add up, creating a significant barrier to entry for many aspiring entrepreneurs. In contrast, vending machines offer a much more affordable path to business ownership.

Purchasing a vending machine can be relatively inexpensive, especially when compared to the costs of setting up a retail space. Depending on the type and features, a vending machine can range from a few hundred to a few thousand dollars. Moreover, once you've acquired the machines, your ongoing expenses are minimal. You don't have to worry about paying rent for a prime location or covering the salaries of numerous employees. Instead, your primary costs revolve around maintaining and stocking the machines. This low overhead allows you to start small and gradually expand your operations as your business grows.

Recurring revenue is another significant advantage of the vending machine business. Unlike other ventures that require constant effort to generate sales, vending machines work for you around the clock. Once your machines are in place and stocked with products, they can generate income 24/7, even while you sleep. This steady stream of revenue is particularly appealing for those looking to create a reliable source of passive income.

Each time a customer purchases an item from one of your vending machines, you're making money without needing to be physically present. This recurring revenue model is especially advantageous because it provides a predictable income stream that can be scaled with relative ease. By strategically placing additional machines in high-traffic areas, you can increase your earnings without a proportional increase in your workload. This scalability is a key factor in the long-term success and growth of a vending machine business.

Often overlooked benefit of running a vending machine business is the work-life balance it offers. Many traditional businesses demand long hours, leaving little time for personal pursuits or family life. However, the vending machine industry provides a level of flexibility that is hard to match. Since vending machines operate independently, you can manage your business on your own schedule.

Routine tasks like restocking machines, collecting payments, and performing maintenance can be scheduled at times that are convenient for you. This flexibility allows you to maintain a healthy balance between work and personal life. Whether you're looking to spend more time with your family, pursue a hobby, or even run another business, vending machines give you the freedom to do so.

Advancements in technology have made managing vending machines even more convenient. Modern machines come equipped with features like remote monitoring, which allows you to check inventory levels and machine performance from your smartphone or computer. This means you can address issues or plan restocking trips without needing to physically inspect each machine. The ability to manage your business remotely further enhances your ability to maintain a balanced lifestyle while ensuring your machines are always in optimal condition.

The vending machine business also offers the opportunity to diversify your income. By offering a variety of products, from snacks and beverages to healthier options and even non-food items like personal care products, you can cater to different markets and customer preferences. This diversification helps to mitigate risk and ensures a steady flow of revenue, even if preferences shift over time.

The initial investment in a vending machine business can be adjusted to fit different budgets and goals. Whether you want to start with a single machine or launch with several, you have the flexibility to scale your investment according to your financial situation and business ambitions. This makes the vending machine industry accessible to a wide range of entrepreneurs, from those seeking a side hustle to those aiming to build a large-scale operation

Unveiling Your Vision

Every successful business starts with a vision, a clear idea of what you want to achieve and why it matters. In the vending machine industry, this vision can be as simple or as grand as you make it, but it's the driving force that guides your decisions and keeps you motivated. For me, the journey into the vending machine business was inspired by a desire to promote healthier snacking options and create a community that values wellness and convenience.

My personal motivation stemmed from my own struggles with finding healthy snacks on the go. As someone who is health-conscious, I often found it challenging to locate nutritious options when I needed a quick bite. Traditional vending machines, stocked primarily with sugary snacks and sodas, offered little in the way of healthy choices. This gap in the market sparked an idea: why not fill vending machines with wholesome, nutritious snacks that cater to the growing demand for healthier food options?

The vision became clear: I wanted to create a network of vending machines that provided convenient access to healthy snacks. But beyond just offering healthier options, I wanted to build a community around this concept. The idea was to foster a sense of connection among like-minded individuals who prioritize health and wellness in their daily lives. This is where social media comes into play, aligning perfectly with my goals.

Social media is a powerful tool that can amplify your message and help you reach a broader audience. For my vending machine business, it serves as a platform to engage with customers, share valuable content, and build a loyal community. Here's how it aligns with and supports my vision:

Educating and Informing:

One of the primary goals of my vending machine business is to educate people about the benefits of healthy snacking. Through social media, I can share informative content about the nutritional value of the products in my machines. Posts about the benefits of nuts, the advantages of low-sugar snacks, or the importance of staying hydrated with healthy beverages can help inform and inspire my audience. Educational content not only adds value to the customer experience but also positions my brand as a trusted source of health information.

Building a Community:

Creating a sense of community is essential for fostering customer loyalty. Social media platforms like Facebook, Instagram, and Twitter allow me to connect with customers on a personal level. By sharing stories, engaging in conversations, and responding to feedback, I can build strong relationships with my audience. Hosting online events, such as Q&A sessions or live chats about health topics, further strengthens these connections and makes customers feel like they are part of a larger movement.

Promoting Products and Locations:

Social media is an excellent channel for promoting the products available in my vending machines and highlighting new locations. Regular updates about new snack options, special promotions, or the introduction of machines in new areas keep the audience informed and excited. Eye-catching photos and engaging videos showcasing the products and their benefits can drive interest and encourage more people to try out the vending machines.

Gathering Customer Feedback:

Feedback is crucial for improving any business. Social media provides a direct line of communication with customers, allowing me to gather insights into their preferences and experiences. Polls, surveys, and open-ended questions can help identify which products are popular and which ones might need to be replaced. Understanding customer preferences ensures that the vending machines are stocked with items that meet their needs, enhancing overall satisfaction.

Encouraging Health Challenges and Engagement:

To further promote healthy living, I can use social media to organize health challenges and campaigns. For instance, a "30-Day Healthy Snack Challenge" where participants commit to choosing healthier snacks from my vending machines can create buzz and drive engagement. Sharing user-generated content, such as photos of customers enjoying their snacks, can also foster a sense of community and inspire others to join in.

Partnering With Influencers:

Collaborating with health and wellness influencers can extend the reach of my brand. Influencers who share the same values and have a substantial following can help promote the vending machines and the healthy products they offer. Their endorsement can add credibility and attract new customers who trust their recommendations.

Leveraging Analytics:

Social media platforms provide valuable analytics that can inform business decisions. By analyzing engagement metrics, audience demographics, and content performance, I can refine my social media strategy to better align with customer interests and preferences. This data-driven approach ensures that my efforts are effective and contribute to the overall growth of the business.

Building Your Vending Machine Business

Initial Investment Breakdown

vending machine business requires careful financial planning to ensure you have a clear understanding of the initial investment needed. Starting costs can vary significantly depending on several factors, including the type of vending machines you choose, the products you plan to offer, and additional supplies and services necessary to get your business up and running. Let's break down these costs to give you a comprehensive overview of what to expect.

Vending Machines:

The cornerstone of your business is, of course, the vending machines themselves. There are several types to consider:

Snack Machines: These machines, designed to dispense various snacks, can range in price from $1,000 to $3,000, depending on the size and features.

Drink Machines: Similar to snack machines, drink vending machines can cost between $1,500 and $4,000. Models that offer both cold and hot beverages tend to be on the higher end.

Combo Machines: These versatile machines can dispense both snacks and drinks. They are typically more expensive, with prices ranging from $2,000 to $5,000.

Specialty Machines: Machines designed to dispense healthier options, frozen items, or non-food products (like electronics) can vary widely in cost, often starting around $3,000 and going up to $10,000.

When budgeting for vending machines, it's important to factor in the number of machines you plan to start with. A common approach is to begin with a few machines to test the market and gradually expand based on demand and profitability.

Inventory:

Stocking your vending machines requires an initial investment in inventory. The cost of inventory will depend on the types of products you choose and the volume you intend to purchase. Here's a rough estimate of initial inventory costs:

Snacks: Purchasing a variety of snacks in bulk can cost between $500 and $1,000 per machine. This includes chips, candy, granola bars, and other popular snack items.

Drinks: Beverages tend to have higher initial costs due to their size and weight. Expect to spend around $800 to $1,200 per machine on drinks such as bottled water, sodas, juices, and energy drinks.

Healthy Options: If you're focusing on healthier products, the cost may be slightly higher. Healthy snacks and drinks often come with a premium price, so budget an additional 10-20% more for these items.

To minimize costs, consider negotiating with suppliers for bulk purchase discounts or looking for wholesale distributors who specialize in vending machine products.

Supplies and Equipment:

Beyond the machines and inventory, you'll need various supplies and equipment to support your business operations:

Payment Systems: Modern vending machines often include cash-less payment systems, such as credit card readers and mobile payment options. These systems can cost between $300 and $600 per machine.

Initial Stocking Supplies: This includes items like shelves, product dividers, and coils necessary to organize products within the machine. Budget around $100 to $200 per machine for these supplies.

Maintenance Tools: Basic tools for routine maintenance and repairs are essential. A toolkit with items like screwdrivers, wrenches, and cleaning supplies might cost around $100.

Transportation: If you're transporting the machines yourself, consider the cost of renting a truck or van. Additionally, you may need dollies or other moving equipment to safely move the machines. Budget around $300 to $500 for initial transportation needs.

Permits and Licenses

Starting a vending machine business typically requires obtaining various permits and licenses, depending on local regulations. These may include:

Business License: A general business license, which can cost between $50 and $200.

Health Permit: If you're selling food and beverages, a health permit from the local health department is often required. This can cost between $50 and $300, depending on your location.

Sales Tax Permit: Registering for a sales tax permit may be necessary, and the cost varies by state but is usually under $100.

Location Fees:

Securing high-traffic locations for your vending machines often involves negotiating placement fees with property owners. These fees can take different forms:

Flat Monthly Fee: Some property owners charge a flat monthly fee for placing your machine on their premises. This can range from $50 to $150 per location.

Revenue Sharing: Alternatively, you may negotiate a revenue-sharing agreement, where you pay the property owner a percentage of the sales. Typically, this ranges from 10% to 25% of monthly revenue.

Marketing and Branding:

Creating a strong brand identity and promoting your business are crucial for attracting customers:

Branding Materials: This includes designing a logo, creating signage for your machines, and printing business cards. Initial costs might be around $200 to $500.

Website and Social Media: Building a website and establishing a social media presence can cost anywhere from $500 to $1,000, depending on whether you hire a professional or do it yourself.

Advertising: Consider initial advertising expenses to promote your vending machines. This could include online ads, flyers, or promotional events, with a budget of around $300 to $700.

Total Initial Investment:

Summing up all these costs, a realistic initial investment for starting a vending machine business with a few machines can range from $5,000 to $15,000. Here's a quick breakdown:

Vending Machines (3 machines): $6,000 - $12,000
Inventory: $2,100 - $3,600
Supplies and Equipment: $800 - $1,400
Permits and Licenses: $150 - $600
Location Fees: $150 - $450
Marketing and Branding: $1,000 - $2,200

By understanding these costs and planning accordingly, you can set a solid foundation for your vending machine business, ensuring you're well-prepared to manage expenses and maximize your chances of success.

Legal and Regulatory Considerations

Starting a vending machine business involves more than just purchasing machines and stocking them with products. To operate legally and avoid potential fines or shutdowns, you must navigate various legal and regulatory requirements. This includes obtaining necessary permits and licenses and understanding the regulations that govern vending machines in your area.

Obtaining Permits and Licenses:

Business License:

Every business, including vending machine operations, typically needs a business license. This license legitimizes your business and allows you to operate within your jurisdiction. The cost and process for obtaining a business license vary by location but generally involve submitting an application to your city or county government and paying a fee.

Health Permit:

Since vending machines often dispense food and beverages, a health permit is usually required. The local health department issues this permit and ensures that your vending machines comply with health and safety standards. The application process may include an inspection of your machines to verify they are clean, well-maintained, and safe for dispensing food.

Sales Tax Permit:

If your state imposes a sales tax, you'll need to register for a sales tax permit. This permit allows you to collect sales tax from customers and remit it to the state. The registration process typically involves providing details about your business and paying a small fee. Once registered, you will need to file regular sales tax returns and keep accurate records of your sales and tax collected.

Vending Machine Permit:

Some jurisdictions require a specific permit for each vending machine. This permit ensures that each machine is registered with the local authorities and complies with all relevant regulations.

Zoning and Land Use Permits:

Before placing vending machines in certain locations, you may need to check local zoning laws and obtain land use permits. These regulations ensure that vending machines are placed in appropriate areas and do not violate any zoning restrictions. This is particularly important for outdoor or public placements.

Understanding Vending Machine Regulations:

Health and Safety Standards:

Health and safety regulations are critical for vending machines that dispense food and beverages. These standards ensure that products are stored and dispensed safely to prevent contamination. Key requirements may include maintaining proper temperature controls, regular cleaning schedules, and ensuring that products are within their expiration dates. Compliance with these regulations is essential to avoid penalties and ensure customer safety.

Accessibility Requirements:

Many jurisdictions have regulations that require vending machines to be accessible to all customers, including those with disabilities. This may involve ensuring that machines are at an appropriate height and have features that accommodate users with disabilities, such as braille instructions or voice assistance. Compliance with the Americans with Disabilities Act (ADA) in the United States, for example, is crucial for avoiding legal issues and ensuring inclusivity.

Product Labeling:

Regulations may also dictate how products within vending machines should be labeled. This includes displaying nutritional information, ingredients, and potential allergens. Proper labeling helps customers make informed choices and ensures transparency about the products being sold.

Advertising and Signage:

Local laws might regulate the advertising and signage on vending machines. This can include restrictions on the size, placement, and content of advertisements. It's important to review these regulations to ensure that your marketing efforts comply with local laws.

Maintenance and Inspection Requirements:

Regular maintenance and inspections are often mandated to ensure that vending machines remain in good working order. This includes keeping machines clean, performing necessary repairs promptly, and maintaining accurate records of maintenance activities. Some jurisdictions may also require periodic inspections by health or safety officials.

Navigating the legal and regulatory landscape for a vending machine business can seem daunting, but it is essential for operating a compliant and successful enterprise. By obtaining the necessary permits and licenses and adhering to local regulations, you can avoid legal pitfalls and build a solid foundation for your business. Taking these steps ensures that your vending machine operation is legally sound and ready to serve customers safely and efficiently.

Building Your Brand Identity:

Developing a Name

Your brand name is the first impression customers will have of your business, so it's essential to choose something memorable and reflective of your mission. Here are some tips for developing a strong brand name:

Reflect Your Vision: Your name should convey what your business stands for. If you're focused on healthy snacks, incorporate words like "nutritious," "fresh," or "health." For a broader appeal, you might choose something more general yet catchy.

Keep It Simple: A simple, easy-to-pronounce name is more likely to stick in customers' minds. Avoid overly complex or lengthy names.

Be Unique: Research existing vending machine businesses to ensure your name stands out. Unique names help avoid confusion and legal issues related to trademarks.

Think Long-Term: Choose a name that will grow with your business. Avoid names that might limit your future expansion into new product lines or markets.

Designing a Logo

A well-designed logo is a visual representation of your brand and plays a significant role in building recognition and trust. Here's how to create an effective logo:

Use Relevant Imagery: Incorporate images or symbols related to vending, snacks, or your specific focus (e.g., healthy options). This helps convey what your business is about at a glance.

Choose the Right Colors: Colors evoke emotions and associations. Use colors that align with your brand's personality – green for health and freshness, red for energy, or blue for trust and reliability.

Ensure Scalability: Your logo should look good at any size, whether it's on a vending machine, social media profile, or business card. Test it in different formats to ensure clarity and legibility.

Establishing a Social Media Presence

A strong social media presence helps you connect with customers, promote your brand, and build a loyal community. Here's how to leverage social media for your vending machine business:

Choose the Right Platforms: Focus on platforms where your target audience is most active. Instagram and Facebook are great for visual content, while Twitter is useful for quick updates and engagement.

Create Engaging Content: Share high-quality images and videos of your products, highlight new locations, and post behind-the-scenes content. Engage with your audience through polls, contests, and Q&A sessions.

Be Consistent: Maintain a consistent posting schedule to keep your audience engaged. Use a content calendar to plan and organize your posts.

Use Hashtags and Keywords: Leverage relevant hashtags and keywords to increase the visibility of your posts. Research trending hashtags related to vending, snacks, and health to reach a broader audience.

Engage With Followers: Respond to comments, messages, and reviews promptly. Showing that you value customer feedback and interaction builds trust and loyalty.

These elements work together to distinguish your vending machine business in the marketplace and attract a dedicated customer base

Chapter 2
Crunching the Numbers: Mastering Profitability

Imagine this: your vending machines are in high-traffic locations, fully stocked with snacks and beverages that customers love. Sales are steady, and you're starting to see a return on your investment. But how do you ensure that this momentum continues? The answer lies in a solid grasp of your finances. By breaking down your costs, setting the right prices, and managing your cash flow, you can create a sustainable business model that not only covers your expenses but also maximizes your profits.

Understanding your finances begins with a clear analysis of your costs. From the initial purchase of vending machines and stocking them with inventory to ongoing expenses like maintenance and repairs, knowing where your money goes is the first step toward controlling your budget. It's not just about cutting costs but also about making smart investments that will pay off in the long run. This chapter will show you how to break down these costs effectively and make informed decisions that support your financial goals.

Pricing your products correctly is another critical factor in achieving profitability. It's a delicate balance: set your prices too high, and you risk scaring off potential customers; set them too low, and you might not cover your costs. We'll explore strategies for calculating the cost of your products, determining the optimal profit margins, and setting competitive prices that attract customers while ensuring a healthy profit. You'll learn how to analyze your sales data and adjust your pricing strategy based on customer demand and market trends.

Understanding Your Finances

Cost Analysis

Running a profitable vending machine business requires a thorough understanding of all the associated costs. Breaking down these expenses helps you budget effectively and ensures you make informed decisions to maximize your profitability. Let's explore the key cost components: the initial purchase of the machines, ongoing maintenance, and potential repairs.

Initial Purchase Costs

The first significant expense in your vending machine business is the purchase of the machines themselves. The cost of a vending machine can vary widely based on several factors, including the type, size, and features. Here's a closer look at the different types of vending machines and their average costs:

Snack Machines:

Price Range: $1,000 to $3,000

These machines dispense a variety of snacks, from chips and candy to granola bars and nuts. They are a staple in the vending industry due to their versatility and popularity.

Drink Machines:

Price Range: $1,500 to $4,000

Drink machines can dispense cold beverages like sodas and bottled water or hot beverages like coffee and tea. Machines that offer both options tend to be on the higher end of the price spectrum.

Combo Machines:

Price Range: $2,000 to $5,000

Combo machines offer the best of both worlds by providing both snacks and drinks. They are convenient for customers and efficient for operators, making them a popular choice despite their higher initial cost.

Specialty Machines:

Price Range: $3,000 to $10,000

These machines cater to niche markets, such as healthy snacks, frozen foods, or even non-food items like electronics and personal care products. Their specialized nature and advanced features often command a higher price.

When budgeting for vending machines, consider starting with a few units and gradually expanding as your business grows. This approach allows you to manage your initial investment and learn the business dynamics before scaling up.

Ongoing Maintenance Costs

Maintaining your vending machines is crucial for ensuring they operate efficiently and provide a positive customer experience. Regular maintenance helps prevent breakdowns, extends the lifespan of your machines, and keeps them looking clean and appealing. Here are the main components of maintenance costs:

Routine Cleaning:

Cost: $10 to $30 per machine per month

Regular cleaning is essential to keep your machines hygienic and attractive. This includes wiping down the exterior, cleaning the dispensing mechanisms, and ensuring the product storage areas are free from debris.

Restocking:

Cost: Variable (based on product prices and frequency of restocking)

Restocking involves replenishing the products in your machines. The cost will depend on the types of products you offer and how frequently your machines need restocking. Efficient route planning can help minimize travel time and fuel expenses.

Software Updates:

Cost: $50 to $200 annually

Many modern vending machines come with software that requires periodic updates. These updates can improve functionality, security, and payment processing capabilities.

Preventive Maintenance:

Cost: $100 to $300 per machine per year

Preventive maintenance includes tasks like inspecting and lubricating mechanical parts, checking electrical components, and ensuring all systems are functioning correctly. Regular preventive maintenance can help avoid costly repairs down the line.

Repair Costs

Despite your best efforts at maintenance, vending machines can still experience breakdowns and require repairs. Being prepared for these unexpected expenses is crucial for maintaining smooth operations. Here are some common repair costs:

Mechanical Repairs:

Cost: $50 to $300 per incident

Mechanical issues, such as jammed dispensing mechanisms or faulty coin acceptors, are common problems. Depending on the complexity of the issue, repair costs can vary.

Electrical Repairs:

Cost: $100 to $500 per incident

Electrical problems, including malfunctioning displays, payment system failures, or lighting issues, often require specialized knowledge to fix. These repairs can be more expensive due to the technical expertise needed.

Component Replacements:

Cost: $50 to $400 per component

Sometimes, individual components like motors, belts, or circuit boards may need replacing. Having a stock of common replacement parts can reduce downtime and service costs.

Professional Service:

Cost: $75 to $150 per hour

If you're unable to handle repairs yourself, hiring a professional technician is necessary. Many vending machine companies offer service contracts that can cover regular maintenance and repairs for a fixed annual fee, which can be a cost-effective option.

Budgeting and Managing Costs

To effectively manage these costs, it's important to create a detailed budget that includes both initial and ongoing expenses. Here are some tips for budgeting and cost management:

Create a Contingency Fund:

Set aside a portion of your budget for unexpected repairs and emergencies. A contingency fund can help you handle sudden expenses without disrupting your cash flow.

Monitor Expenses Regularly:

Keep track of all maintenance and repair costs to identify patterns and potential areas for cost savings. Regular monitoring helps you stay on top of your finances and make informed decisions.

Negotiate With Suppliers:

Building good relationships with your vending machine suppliers and service providers can lead to better prices and terms. Don't hesitate to negotiate bulk purchase discounts or service contract rates.

Invest in Quality:

While it might be tempting to opt for cheaper machines or parts, investing in quality equipment can save money in the long run by reducing the frequency of repairs and extending the lifespan of your machines.

By understanding and carefully managing the costs associated with purchasing, maintaining, and repairing vending machines, you can ensure your business operates efficiently and profitably. This proactive approach to cost management is essential for long-term success in the vending machine industry.

Product Costing and Pricing Strategies:

Achieving profitability in your vending machine business hinges on effective product costing and pricing strategies. Calculating the cost of your products, setting appropriate profit margins, and determining competitive pricing are essential steps to ensure your business remains viable and attractive to customers. Here's how to navigate these critical financial aspects.

Calculating Product Cost

Understanding the true cost of the products you stock is the first step in setting prices that ensure profitability. Product cost includes several components:

Purchase Price:

This is the amount you pay to acquire the products from suppliers. Buying in bulk can often reduce the per-unit cost, so it's beneficial to negotiate bulk purchase deals with your suppliers.

Shipping and Handling:

Include any shipping and handling fees charged by suppliers. These costs can add up, especially if you're sourcing products from multiple vendors or distant locations.

Storage:

If you need to store products before they are placed in vending machines, factor in the cost of storage facilities. This might include rent for warehouse space, utilities, and storage equipment.

Spoilage and Waste:

Not all products will sell before they expire, leading to some wastage. Estimate a percentage of product loss due to spoilage and incorporate this into your overall product cost.

To calculate the total product cost per unit, add up these components. For example, if you purchase a case of 100 snack bars for $100, pay $20 for shipping, and estimate $10 for spoilage, the total cost is $130. Dividing this by 100 units gives a per-unit cost of $1.30.

Setting Profit Margins

Once you know your product costs, the next step is to determine your desired profit margin. Profit margin is the difference between the cost of the product and the price at which you sell it, expressed as a percentage of the selling price. Here's how to set profit margins:

Determine Desired Profit Margin:

A common target in the vending machine industry is a profit margin of 50-100%. This means if your product cost is $1.30, you would aim to sell it for $1.95 to $2.60.

Calculate Selling Price:

To calculate the selling price, use the formula:

> Selling Price=Product Cost×(1+Desired Profit Margin)
> For example, with a product cost of $1.30 and a desired profit margin of 50%, the selling price would be:
> $\{$Selling Price$\} = \$1.30 \times (1 + 0.50) = \$1.95$

Adjust for Market Conditions:

It's essential to consider market conditions and customer expectations when setting your prices. If your competition offers similar products at lower prices, you may need to adjust your margins to remain competitive while still ensuring profitability.

Competitive Pricing

Competitive pricing ensures that your products are attractively priced in the market. Here are steps to develop a competitive pricing strategy:

Market Research:

Analyze prices of similar products in other vending machines in your area. This helps you understand the price range customers are willing to pay and identify gaps where you can position your products competitively.

Value Proposition:

Differentiate your offerings based on value rather than just price. For example, if you offer healthier snack options or premium products, customers may be willing to pay a higher price. Highlighting these unique selling points can justify higher prices.

Dynamic Pricing:

Consider implementing dynamic pricing strategies where you adjust prices based on demand, location, and seasonality. For instance, you might charge higher prices in high-traffic locations or during peak times.

Promotions and Discounts:

Offer periodic promotions, discounts, or bundle deals to attract customers and boost sales. This can help you clear slow-moving inventory and increase overall revenue.

Monitor and Adjust:

Regularly review your pricing strategy and sales data. Adjust prices based on customer feedback, sales performance, and changes in supplier costs. Flexibility in pricing helps you stay competitive and responsive to market trends..

Utilizing Social Media Analytics:

Social media platforms like Facebook, Instagram, Twitter, and LinkedIn offer built-in analytics tools that provide a wealth of data about your followers and audience. Here's how you can utilize these tools to understand your customer demographics:

Age and Gender:

Social media analytics reveal the age and gender distribution of your audience. Knowing the predominant age groups and gender of your followers helps tailor your product offerings and pricing. For instance, if your audience is primarily young adults, you might focus on trendy, healthy snacks that appeal to health-conscious consumers.

Location:

Geographic data shows where your followers are located. This information is crucial for placing your vending machines in high-demand areas. Additionally, understanding the economic status of different locations can help you set prices that are competitive yet profitable. Higher-income areas might support higher prices, while in lower-income areas, competitive pricing is essential.

Interests and Preferences:

Social media platforms track the interests and behaviors of users. By analyzing this data, you can identify trends and preferences among your audience. For example, if you find a significant portion of your audience is interested in fitness and wellness, stocking your machines with protein bars, energy drinks, and other health-oriented products can be a winning strategy.

Engagement Metrics:

Engagement metrics such as likes, comments, shares, and clicks provide insights into what content resonates most with your audience. High engagement on posts about certain products can indicate strong interest and demand, informing both product selection and pricing strategies.

Applying Insights to Pricing Strategies

Once you have gathered and analyzed social media data, you can apply these insights to your pricing strategies:

Segmented Pricing:

Use demographic data to implement segmented pricing strategies. For example, if you have vending machines in various locations, tailor the pricing based on the demographic data of each location. Higher-income areas might bear higher prices, while you might offer lower prices or discounts in price-sensitive regions.

Promotional Offers:

Create targeted promotional offers based on customer interests and behaviors. If social media analytics show a high engagement with posts about new product launches, consider offering introductory discounts to boost initial sales and gather further data on product performance.

Product Bundling:

Insights into customer preferences can help you create appealing product bundles. For example, if your audience shows a preference for healthy snacks and beverages, offer bundled deals that combine these products at a slight discount, encouraging higher sales volumes and increasing overall revenue.

Dynamic Pricing:

Use social media insights to implement dynamic pricing strategies, adjusting prices based on real-time demand and engagement. For instance, if a particular product gains sudden popularity on social media, you can adjust its price to maximize profits while the demand is high.

Feedback Loop:

Encourage customers to provide feedback on social media about pricing and product satisfaction. Use this direct feedback loop to make informed adjustments to your pricing strategies, ensuring they align with customer expectations and market trends.

Utilizing social media analytics is a strategic way to understand your customer demographics and tailor your pricing strategies accordingly.. Embracing these tools not only keeps you connected with your customers but also positions your business for sustained success in a competitive market..

Projecting Success: Building a Financial Roadmap

Revenue Streams and Sales Forecasting

Building a successful vending machine business requires a clear understanding of your revenue streams and the ability to accurately forecast sales. This involves identifying and optimizing various sources of income, such as snacks and drinks, and using data-driven methods to project potential sales. By doing so, you can create a robust financial roadmap that guides your business towards sustained profitability and growth.

Exploring Different Revenue Streams

A diverse range of revenue streams is crucial for maximizing the profitability of your vending machine business. Here are the primary revenue streams to consider:

Snacks:

Traditional Snacks: Items like chips, candy bars, and cookies are staple products in vending machines. These items typically have high turnover rates and appeal to a wide audience.

Healthy Snacks: With increasing health consciousness, offering options like granola bars, nuts, dried fruits, and low-calorie snacks can attract health-minded consumers and differentiate your vending machines from competitors.

Drinks:

Beverages: This category includes sodas, bottled water, juices, and energy drinks. Drinks often generate higher sales volumes due to their necessity and convenience.

Specialty Drinks: Healthier drink options such as flavored water, sports drinks, and organic beverages cater to niche markets and can command higher prices.

Additional Product Offerings:

Fresh Food:

Some vending machines are equipped to offer fresh food items like sandwiches, salads, and fruit cups. These products can attract office workers and students looking for quick meal options.

Non-Food Items:

Depending on the location, vending machines can also dispense items like personal care products, electronics accessories, and office supplies. This can be particularly effective in locations like gyms, airports, and offices.

Sales Forecasting

Accurate sales forecasting is essential for planning inventory, managing cash flow, and setting realistic financial goals. Here's how to forecast sales effectively for your vending machine business:

Historical Sales Data:

If you have existing machines, analyze past sales data to identify trends and patterns. Look at factors such as peak sales periods, seasonal variations, and the performance of different products. This historical data provides a baseline for future projections.

Market Research:

Conduct market research to understand consumer preferences and demand in different locations. This can involve surveys, focus groups, and analyzing competitors. Understanding the market helps you predict which products will perform well and how to price them competitively.

Location Analysis:

The success of a vending machine largely depends on its location. High-traffic areas like office buildings, schools, gyms, and hospitals tend to generate higher sales. Evaluate potential locations based on foot traffic, demographics, and competition. Use this information to estimate sales volumes for each location.

Product Mix Optimization:

Diversifying your product offerings based on customer preferences can boost sales. For example, offering a mix of traditional and healthy snacks or adding seasonal items can attract a broader customer base. Regularly updating your product mix keeps the selection fresh and appealing, encouraging repeat purchases.

Economic Indicators:

Consider broader economic indicators that might impact consumer spending, such as inflation rates, employment levels, and disposable income. Economic downturns might reduce spending on non-essential items, while economic growth can boost sales.

Promotional Activities:

Factor in the impact of promotions and marketing campaigns. Discounts, special offers, and new product launches can temporarily boost sales. Plan these activities strategically to coincide with high-traffic periods or seasonal trends.

Creating a Sales Forecast

To create a sales forecast, follow these steps:

Set Time Frames:

Determine the period for your forecast, such as monthly, quarterly, or annually. Shorter time frames allow for more precise adjustments, while longer periods provide a broader view of trends.

Estimate Sales Volumes:

Based on your historical data, market research, and location analysis, estimate the sales volume for each product category in each vending machine location. Consider peak times and seasonal variations.

Calculate Revenue:

Multiply the estimated sales volume by the selling price of each product to calculate the total revenue for each category. Sum these figures to get the overall revenue projection for each time frame.

Adjust for Variables:

Adjust your forecast for potential variables such as changes in consumer preferences, economic shifts, and competitive actions. Regularly review and update your forecast to reflect new data and trends..

Cash Flow Management

Cash flow is the movement of money in and out of your business, and managing it well ensures that you have sufficient liquidity to cover expenses, invest in growth opportunities, and handle unexpected costs. Here are strategies to help you manage your cash flow effectively.

Understanding Cash Flow

Cash flow consists of two main components: incoming cash (inflows) and outgoing cash (outflows).

Incoming Cash (Inflows):

Sales Revenue: The primary source of cash inflow is the revenue generated from vending machine sales. This includes the money collected from the sale of snacks, drinks, and other products.

Additional Income: Other sources of income might include interest on savings, rebates from suppliers, and income from advertising if you allow ads on your machines.

Outgoing Cash (Outflows):

Inventory Purchases: Regular expenditure on purchasing snacks, drinks, and other products to stock your vending machines.

Maintenance and Repairs: Costs related to maintaining and repairing vending machines to keep them in good working condition.

Operational Expenses: These include expenses such as rent for storage spaces, utilities, transportation costs for restocking, and salaries if you employ staff.

Administrative Costs: Expenses related to business operations, such as permits, licenses, insurance, and office supplies.

Strategies for Managing Cash Flow

Monitor Cash Flow Regularly:

Keep a close eye on your cash flow by tracking all incoming and outgoing transactions. Use accounting software to generate cash flow statements regularly. This helps you understand your cash position and identify trends or potential issues early.

Forecast Cash Flow:

Create cash flow forecasts to predict your future cash needs. Forecasting involves estimating your inflows and outflows over a specific period, such as monthly or quarterly. This proactive approach helps you anticipate cash shortages and plan accordingly.

Maintain a Cash Reserve:

Set aside a portion of your earnings as a cash reserve to cover unexpected expenses or downturns in sales. A cash reserve acts as a financial safety net, allowing you to manage unforeseen costs without disrupting your operations.

Optimize Inventory Management:

Efficient inventory management ensures that you have the right amount of stock to meet customer demand without overstocking, which ties up cash. Use inventory management software to track stock levels, sales trends, and reorder points. This helps you make informed purchasing decisions and reduce excess inventory costs.

Negotiate Favorable Terms With Suppliers:

Establish good relationships with your suppliers and negotiate favorable payment terms. For example, negotiate longer payment terms to delay outflows or request discounts for early payments or bulk purchases. Favorable terms can improve your cash flow by reducing immediate cash outlays.

Manage Receivables Efficiently:

If you offer vending services on a contract basis to businesses or institutions, ensure timely collection of receivables. Set clear payment terms and follow up promptly on overdue invoices. Efficient receivables management ensures that you have a steady inflow of cash.

Control Operational Expenses:

Review your operational expenses regularly and identify areas where you can cut costs without compromising quality. This might include negotiating lower rent for storage spaces, optimizing delivery routes to save on fuel, or reducing utility costs.

Leverage Technology:

Use cashless payment systems in your vending machines to improve cash flow. Cashless payments reduce the time and cost associated with collecting and counting cash, minimize the risk of theft, and provide immediate access to funds.

Plan for Seasonality:

Recognize and plan for seasonal fluctuations in sales. For example, vending machine sales may be higher in schools during the academic year and lower during holidays. Adjust your inventory and cash flow management strategies to account for these variations.

Seek Financing Options:

If you anticipate a cash flow shortfall, consider short-term financing options such as business lines of credit, loans, or factoring receivables. These options can provide the necessary liquidity to bridge gaps in cash flow.

Break-Even Analysis: Calculating the Point at Which Your Business Becomes Profitable.

A break-even analysis helps you determine the point at which your total revenues equal your total costs, meaning you are neither making a profit nor incurring a loss. Knowing this point allows you to plan effectively and strategize for growth. Here's how to conduct a break-even analysis for your vending machine business.

Components of Break-Even Analysis

To perform a break-even analysis, you need to understand and calculate three key components:

Fixed Costs (FC):

These are costs that do not change regardless of the number of vending machines or the volume of products sold. Fixed costs include expenses such as:

- Purchase or lease payments for vending machines
- Insurance
- Licenses and permits
- Storage rental fees
- Salaries (if you employ staff)

Variable Costs (VC):

These costs vary directly with the volume of products sold. Variable costs include:

- Cost of goods sold (COGS) for snacks, drinks, and other products
- Restocking costs
- Transaction fees for cashless payment systems

Sales Revenue (SR):

This is the income generated from selling products in your vending machines. It depends on the price at which you sell each product and the number of products sold.

Calculating the Break-Even Point

The break-even point (BEP) is calculated using the following formula:

Break-Even Point (Units)=Fixed Costs Selling Price per Unit−Variable Cost per Unit

Break-Even Point (Units)= Selling Price per Unit−Variable Cost per Unit Fixed Costs

Here's a step-by-step guide to calculating the break-even point:

Determine Fixed Costs:

List all your fixed costs. For example:

- Lease payments for five vending machines: $500/month
- Insurance: $100/month
- Licenses and permits: $50/month
- Storage rental: $200/month
- Total Fixed Costs (FC): $850/month

Calculate Variable Costs per Unit:

Calculate the variable cost per unit for each product. For example, if you stock a snack that costs $1 to purchase and incurs $0.10 in restocking and transaction fees, the variable cost per unit is $1.10.

Set the Selling Price per Unit:

Determine the selling price for each product. If you sell the snack for $2, then:

Selling Price per Unit (SP): $2

Calculate the Contribution Margin per Unit:

The contribution margin is the difference between the selling price and the variable cost per unit. Using our example:

Contribution Margin per Unit (CM) = $2 (SP) - $1.10 (VC) = $0.90

Calculate the Break-Even Point:

Use the formula to calculate the number of units you need to sell to break even:

$$\{\text{Break-Even Point (Units)}\} = \frac{\$850}{0.90} \approx 945 \ \{\text{units}\}$$

This means you need to sell approximately 945 units of the snack each month to cover your fixed and variable costs.

Practical Application

Understanding your break-even point helps you make strategic decisions. Here's how you can use this information:

Pricing Strategy:

Knowing your break-even point allows you to evaluate whether your current pricing strategy is sufficient to cover costs and achieve profitability. If your break-even point is too high, consider adjusting prices or finding ways to reduce variable costs.

Sales Targets:

Set realistic sales targets based on your break-even analysis. If your target locations or customer base seem unlikely to meet these sales figures, you may need to reconsider your business model or marketing strategy.

Cost Management:

Identify areas where you can reduce fixed or variable costs. For instance, negotiating better prices with suppliers or finding more cost-effective storage solutions can lower your break-even point.

Location Selection:

Use break-even analysis to evaluate potential locations for your vending machines. High-traffic areas with higher sales potential can help you reach your break-even point more quickly.

Growth Planning:

As your business grows, continue to update your break-even analysis to reflect changes in fixed and variable costs. This ongoing assessment ensures that you remain on track towards profitability.

Conducting a break-even analysis is a vital step in managing your vending machine business. By calculating the point at which your revenues cover your costs, you can make informed decisions about pricing, sales targets, and cost management. This analysis provides a clear financial roadmap, helping you strategize effectively and move towards sustained profitability and growth. Understanding your break-even point empowers you to plan for success and navigate the financial challenges of running a vending machine business.

Chapter 3
Maximizing Efficiency: Streamlining Operations

Running a vending machine business is about more than just filling machines with products and collecting cash. To truly thrive in this industry, you need to focus on operational efficiency. Streamlining your operations not only boosts your bottom line but also enhances customer satisfaction, ensuring that your machines are always stocked and functioning optimally. In this chapter, we'll dive into the strategies and techniques that will help you maximize efficiency and streamline your vending machine operations.

Imagine a vending machine business where every aspect runs like a well-oiled machine. Your inventory is always up-to-date, your routes are optimized for minimal travel time, and your machines are maintained proactively to avoid downtime. Achieving this level of efficiency requires careful planning, the right tools, and a proactive approach to problem-solving.

Building a Reliable System

Inventory Management Strategies

Proper stock control methods not only ensure that your machines are always well-stocked with popular items but also help minimize waste and maximize profitability. Implementing effective inventory management strategies can lead to significant cost savings, improved customer satisfaction, and streamlined operations. Here's how to achieve efficient stock control in your vending machine business.

Understanding the Importance of Inventory Management

Inventory management involves keeping track of the products stocked in your vending machines, monitoring sales trends, and ensuring timely restocking. Effective inventory management helps you:

Reduce Waste: By monitoring stock levels and sales patterns, you can avoid overstocking and minimize the risk of products expiring or becoming unsellable.

Increase Sales: Ensuring that popular items are always available keeps customers satisfied and encourages repeat purchases.

Optimize Cash Flow: Efficient stock control means less money tied up in unsold inventory, freeing up cash for other business needs.

Improve Efficiency: Streamlined inventory processes reduce the time and effort required for restocking and managing stock levels.

Implementing Efficient Stock Control Methods

Utilize Inventory Management Software:

Modern inventory management software provides real-time data on stock levels, sales trends, and product performance. These tools can automate many aspects of inventory management, such as generating restocking alerts and producing detailed sales reports.

Choose a software solution that integrates with your vending machines and provides insights into inventory turnover rates, which products are selling fast, and which items are slow movers.

Conduct Regular Inventory Audits:

Schedule regular audits to verify actual stock levels against your records. This helps identify discrepancies caused by theft, spoilage, or mismanagement.

Use these audits to adjust your inventory counts and refine your stock control processes. Regular audits ensure that your records are accurate and reliable.

Implement Just-in-Time (JIT) Inventory:

The JIT inventory approach involves stocking products just before they are needed, reducing the amount of inventory held at any given time. This method minimizes waste and ensures fresh products are always available.

Work closely with suppliers to ensure timely deliveries and maintain a flexible restocking schedule that aligns with sales patterns.

Analyze Sales Data:

Regularly analyze sales data to understand which products are popular and which are underperforming. Use this information to make informed decisions about which items to stock and how much inventory to maintain.

Identify peak sales periods and adjust your inventory levels accordingly. For example, certain products may sell better during specific seasons or events, and stocking up in advance can meet increased demand.

Optimize Product Mix:

Offer a balanced mix of products that cater to different tastes and preferences. Include a variety of snacks, drinks, and healthier options to attract a broader customer base.

Regularly review and update your product offerings based on sales performance and customer feedback. Removing underperforming items and introducing new, popular products can boost sales and reduce waste.

Monitor Expiry Dates:

Keep track of product expiry dates to ensure that items are sold before they become unsellable. Arrange products in the machine so that items with the earliest expiration dates are sold first.

Use inventory management software to set alerts for upcoming expiry dates, allowing you to run promotions or discounts to clear stock before it spoils.

Implement Par Levels:

Par levels are the minimum and maximum amounts of each product you want to keep in stock. Setting par levels helps maintain consistent inventory without overstocking.

Adjust par levels based on sales data and seasonal trends. Regularly review and update these levels to reflect changes in customer demand.

Develop Strong Supplier Relationships:

Build strong relationships with reliable suppliers to ensure timely deliveries and favorable terms. Good communication with suppliers can help you manage inventory more effectively and respond quickly to changes in demand.

Negotiate bulk purchase discounts and flexible return policies to minimize waste and reduce costs.

Route Optimization for Efficiency

You can minimize travel time, reduce operational costs, and ensure that your machines are restocked and maintained regularly. This leads to improved customer satisfaction and higher profitability.

Understanding the Importance of Route Optimization

Optimizing your vending machine routes involves strategically planning the sequence and frequency of your visits to each machine. The benefits include:

Reduced Travel Time and Costs: Efficient routes minimize the distance traveled, saving on fuel costs and vehicle wear and tear.

Increased Service Frequency: Well-planned routes enable more frequent visits to high-traffic machines, ensuring they are always stocked and operational.

Improved Time Management: Optimizing routes helps you make the best use of your time, allowing you to service more machines within a given period.

Enhanced Customer Satisfaction: Regularly serviced machines with minimal downtime lead to higher customer satisfaction and increased sales.

Steps to Optimize Your Vending Machine Routes

Analyze Your Current Routes:

Begin by analyzing your existing routes and identifying inefficiencies. Track the time and distance traveled for each route and note any patterns or areas for improvement.

Use this data to establish a baseline and identify opportunities to consolidate or re-sequence stops.

Prioritize High-Traffic Locations:

Identify your highest-traffic vending machines—those that generate the most sales and require more frequent restocking. Prioritize these locations in your route planning to ensure they are serviced regularly.

Use sales data and customer feedback to determine which machines need more frequent attention.

Group Locations Geographically:

Organize your vending machines into geographic clusters to minimize travel distance between stops. Grouping machines located near each other reduces travel time and allows for more efficient servicing.

Plan routes that cover each geographic cluster systematically, reducing backtracking and unnecessary driving.

Utilize Route Planning Software:

Invest in route planning software that uses algorithms to optimize your service routes. These tools can analyze multiple factors, such as traffic patterns, road conditions, and distance, to generate the most efficient routes.

Route planning software can also provide real-time updates and reroute suggestions based on current traffic conditions, helping you avoid delays.

Consider Time Windows:

Some locations may have specific time windows for servicing, such as office buildings or schools that prefer deliveries during off-peak hours. Incorporate these time windows into your route planning to ensure compliance and minimize disruptions.

Balancing time windows with route efficiency requires careful planning but can lead to smoother operations and happier clients.

Optimize Restocking Frequency:

Determine the optimal restocking frequency for each machine based on sales data and product turnover rates. High-traffic machines may need daily visits, while others might only require weekly servicing.

Adjust your routes to match the restocking frequency of each machine, ensuring that no machine runs out of popular products.

Implement Predictive Maintenance:

Use predictive maintenance techniques to anticipate potential machine malfunctions and service them proactively. Route planning software can integrate maintenance schedules into your service routes, allowing you to address issues before they lead to downtime.

Regular maintenance visits can be combined with restocking trips to further optimize routes and reduce travel.

Evaluate and Adjust Regularly:

Route optimization is not a one-time task. Regularly review and evaluate your routes to identify new inefficiencies or changes in traffic patterns. Use sales data and feedback to make informed adjustments.

Flexibility and continuous improvement are key to maintaining optimal routes over time.

Leverage Technology and Data:

Utilize telematics and GPS tracking to monitor your service vehicles in real-time. This technology provides valuable data on travel times, fuel consumption, and route efficiency.

Analyze this data to identify trends and areas for improvement, making adjustments as needed to enhance route efficiency.

Social Media for Customer Service

Strategies for Effective Social Media Customer Service

Monitor Your Social Media Channels:

Regularly monitor your social media accounts for customer messages, comments, and mentions. Use social media management tools to streamline this process and ensure no customer inquiry goes unnoticed.

Set up alerts for mentions of your brand, so you can promptly respond to any issues or questions raised by customers.

Respond Promptly and Professionally:

Aim to respond to customer inquiries and complaints as quickly as possible. A prompt response shows that you value your customers and are attentive to their needs.

Maintain a professional and courteous tone in all interactions, even when addressing complaints. Acknowledge the issue, apologize for any inconvenience, and provide a clear solution or next steps.

Provide Clear and Helpful Information:

When responding to inquiries, provide detailed and helpful information. For example, if a customer asks about the availability of a particular product, offer specifics about which machines stock the item and any upcoming restocking dates.

For complaints, offer actionable solutions. If a machine malfunction is reported, assure the customer that a technician will be dispatched promptly and provide an estimated resolution time.

Use Direct Messaging for Sensitive Issues:

While public responses can demonstrate transparency, some issues may require more privacy. Use direct messaging (DM) to address sensitive or complex matters. This approach allows for a more personalized and detailed resolution.

Follow up with the customer publicly to confirm that the issue is being handled, showing other customers that you take all concerns seriously.

Create a Dedicated Customer Service Handle:

Consider creating a separate social media handle specifically for customer service inquiries (e.g., @YourBrandSupport). This helps streamline customer interactions and ensures that service-related messages receive prompt attention.

Promote this handle across your primary social media channels and vending machines to direct customers to the appropriate place for assistance.

Leverage FAQs and Automated Responses:

Use the FAQ sections on social media platforms to provide quick answers to common questions. This can reduce the volume of inquiries and help customers find information independently.

Implement automated responses to acknowledge receipt of inquiries and let customers know when they can expect a personalized response.

Encourage Customer Feedback:

Actively solicit feedback from customers about their experiences with your vending machines. Use polls, surveys, and open-ended questions to gather insights and identify areas for improvement.

Show appreciation for positive feedback and address any negative feedback constructively, demonstrating your commitment to continuous improvement.

Analyze Customer Interactions:

Regularly review customer interactions on social media to identify trends and common issues. Use this data to improve your products, services, and customer service processes.

Share insights with your team to ensure everyone is aware of recurring problems and can contribute to developing effective solution.

Maintaining Your Vending Machines

Preventive Maintenance Schedule

Preventive maintenance is crucial to ensuring that your vending machines operate smoothly, remain attractive to customers, and minimize downtime. Establishing a comprehensive preventive maintenance schedule that includes regular cleaning, timely restocking, and proactive troubleshooting can significantly enhance the reliability and lifespan of your machines. Here's how to create and implement an effective preventive maintenance routine.

Importance of Preventive Maintenance

Regular preventive maintenance helps to:

- *Reduce Downtime:* Proactively addressing potential issues before they cause machine breakdowns.
- *Enhance Customer Experience:* Ensuring machines are always clean, well-stocked, and operational.

- *Extend Machine Lifespan:* Keeping machines in good working order to avoid costly repairs or replacements.
- *Ensure Compliance*: Meeting health and safety regulations by maintaining hygienic conditions.

Establishing a Preventive Maintenance Schedule

Cleaning Routines

Daily Cleaning:

- Wipe down the exterior surfaces of the machines to remove dust, fingerprints, and spills. A clean machine is more inviting to customers and helps maintain a professional appearance.
- Check for and remove any litter or debris around the machine area.

Weekly Cleaning:

- Clean the dispensing area, including the slots and trays, to prevent residue buildup that could affect the dispensing mechanism.
- Inspect and clean the coin and bill acceptors to ensure they function correctly and to prevent jams.

Monthly Cleaning:

- Conduct a thorough cleaning of the interior components, including shelves and storage areas. Remove all products and clean the surfaces with a mild disinfectant to maintain hygiene.
- Check and clean the refrigeration units in machines that dispense cold beverages or perishable items to ensure they maintain proper temperatures.

Restocking Routines

Monitor Inventory Levels:

- Use inventory management software to track product levels and sales trends. Set alerts for low stock levels to prompt timely restocking.
- Regularly review sales data to adjust restocking frequencies based on demand, ensuring popular items are always available.

Scheduled Restocking:

- Establish a restocking schedule based on machine location and sales volume. High-traffic locations may require daily or bi-weekly restocking, while lower-traffic areas might need weekly restocking.
- Rotate products during restocking to ensure older items are sold first, minimizing the risk of expired products.

Troubleshooting and Inspections

Daily Inspections:

- Perform a quick visual inspection of each machine during restocking visits. Look for signs of wear, damage, or malfunctions.
- Test the machine's functionality by purchasing an item to ensure it dispenses correctly and the payment system works.

Weekly Inspections:

- Check for software updates or firmware upgrades for

digital vending machines. Keeping software up to date can enhance performance and security.

- Inspect the machine's internal components, such as motors, belts, and sensors, to identify any early signs of wear or malfunction.

Monthly Inspections:

- Conduct a more thorough inspection of the electrical and mechanical systems. Look for loose wires, worn parts, or any components that may need lubrication or adjustment.
- Verify that refrigeration units are operating efficiently, maintaining the correct temperatures for perishable products.

Documenting Maintenance Activities

Maintenance Logs:

- Maintain detailed logs of all maintenance activities, including cleaning, restocking, and troubleshooting efforts. Record dates, actions taken, and any issues identified and resolved.
- Use digital tools or software to streamline record-keeping and ensure easy access to maintenance history for each machine.

Regular Reviews:

- Review maintenance logs regularly to identify patterns or recurring issues. Use this information to refine your preventive maintenance schedule and address persistent problems more effectively.

Training and Responsibilities

Staff Training:

- Train your staff on proper cleaning techniques, restocking procedures, and basic troubleshooting skills. Ensure they understand the importance of preventive maintenance and follow the established routines.

Assign Responsibilities:

- Assign specific maintenance tasks to designated team members. Clear responsibilities ensure accountability and consistency in maintenance activities.

Proactive Problem-Solving

Early Detection:

- Encourage staff to report any unusual noises, delays in dispensing, or other signs of potential problems immediately. Early detection allows for timely intervention and prevents minor issues from escalating.

Regular Updates:

- Stay informed about common vending machine issues and solutions. Regularly update your maintenance protocols based on industry best practices and manufacturer recommendations.

Identifying Common Vending Machine Problems

Running a vending machine business involves more than just stocking products and collecting cash; it also requires dealing with occasional malfunctions. Understanding common vending machine problems and knowing basic troubleshooting tips can help you maintain smooth operations and keep your machines in top working condition. Here are some typical issues you might encounter and practical solutions to address them.

Common Vending Machine Problems and Troubleshooting Tips

Coin and Bill Jams

Problem: Customers report that the machine is not accepting coins or bills, or they get stuck. Troubleshooting Tips:

- Check for Obstructions: Open the coin and bill acceptors and remove any foreign objects or debris that may be causing the jam.
- Clean the Acceptors: Use a soft cloth and a mild cleaning solution to clean the coin slots and bill acceptors. Regular cleaning prevents dirt and grime buildup that can cause jams.
- Reset the Machine: Sometimes, a simple reset can resolve the issue. Turn the machine off and on again to see if it resets the coin and bill acceptors.

Product Jams

Problem: Products get stuck and do not dispense properly when selected. Troubleshooting Tips:

- Check the Spiral Coils: Ensure that the spiral coils holding the products are not bent or misaligned. Adjust them if necessary to ensure smooth dispensing.
- Restock Correctly: Avoid overloading the machine, and ensure products are placed correctly in the slots. Overloaded or improperly placed items can cause jams.

- Test Dispensing: After restocking, test the machine by purchasing a product to ensure it dispenses correctly.

Machine Not Dispensing Correct Change

Problem: Customers receive incorrect change or no change at all. Troubleshooting Tips:

- Inspect the Coin Mechanism: Check for any blockages or malfunctions in the coin mechanism. Remove any coins that may be stuck.
- Replenish Coin Supply: Ensure that the machine has an adequate supply of coins for making change. Refill the coin tubes if necessary.
- Calibrate the Coin Mechanism: Some machines require regular calibration to ensure accurate change dispensing. Follow the manufacturer's instructions for calibration.

Display Issues

Problem: The machine's display is not working or showing error messages. Troubleshooting Tips:

- Check Power Supply: Ensure the machine is properly plugged in and receiving power. A loose connection can cause display issues.
- Reset the Machine: Turn the machine off and on to reset the display. This can often resolve minor glitches.
- Consult the Manual: Refer to the machine's manual for specific error codes and troubleshooting steps. Follow the recommended actions to resolve display errors.

Temperature Control Problems

Problem: Refrigerated vending machines are not cooling properly. Troubleshooting Tips:

- Check the Thermostat: Ensure the thermostat is set to the correct temperature. Adjust it if necessary.
- Inspect the Cooling Unit: Make sure the cooling unit is clean and free of dust and debris. Clean the condenser coils regularly to maintain efficiency.
- Ensure Proper Ventilation: Ensure that the machine has adequate ventilation and is not placed too close to walls or other objects that could block airflow.

Electrical Issues

Problem: The machine is not powering on or has intermittent power issues. Troubleshooting Tips:

- Check the Power Cord: Ensure the power cord is securely plugged in and not damaged. Replace the cord if it shows signs of wear.
- Inspect Circuit Breakers: Check the circuit breakers or fuses to ensure they have not tripped or blown. Reset or replace them if necessary.
- Test the Outlet: Use a different device to test the outlet to ensure it is providing power. If the outlet is faulty, contact an electrician for repairs.

Building Partnerships With Repair Technicians

One of the keys to maintaining a successful vending machine business is ensuring your machines are always in working order. To achieve this, you need reliable repair technicians who can provide prompt and effective service. Building strong partnerships with these professionals can minimize downtime, ensuring your machines remain operational and your customers stay satisfied. Here's how to establish and maintain these crucial relationships.

Finding Reliable Technicians

Start by identifying skilled and experienced vending machine repair technicians in your area. Look for professionals who specialize in the types of machines you operate, whether they are snack, beverage, or specialty vending machines. Use the following methods to find reliable technicians:

- *Industry Referrals:* Ask other vending machine operators for recommendations. Industry colleagues can provide valuable insights into the reliability and quality of service of various technicians.
- *Online Reviews and Directories:* Check online business directories and review platforms for highly-rated technicians. Look for feedback from other clients to gauge the technician's reputation and service quality.
- *Manufacturer Recommendations:* Many vending machine manufacturers provide a list of certified repair technicians. These technicians are trained specifically for their machines, ensuring they have the necessary expertise.

Establishing a Partnership

Once you've identified potential technicians, focus on building a strong working relationship with them. This involves clear communication, mutual respect, and establishing expectations. Here's how to establish an effective partnership:

- *Set Clear Expectations:* Clearly outline the scope of work, response times, and service standards you expect from the technician. Discuss availability for emergency repairs and regular maintenance schedules.
- *Negotiate Service Agreements:* Create formal service agreements that detail the terms of the partnership,

including pricing, payment terms, and service commitments. Having a written agreement helps prevent misunderstandings and ensures both parties are on the same page.

- *Regular Communication:* Maintain open lines of communication. Regularly update your technicians on the status of your machines and any recurring issues you've observed. Good communication ensures that technicians are well-prepared for repairs and maintenance.

Benefits of Strong Technician Partnerships

Having a reliable repair technician on call provides several advantages for your vending machine business:

- *Minimized Downtime***:** Quick response times for repairs mean your machines experience less downtime. This ensures continuous service for your customers and maintains your revenue stream.
- *Preventive Maintenance:* Regular maintenance by skilled technicians can prevent many issues before they cause breakdowns. This proactive approach extends the lifespan of your machines and reduces long-term costs.
- *Expert Troubleshooting:* Experienced technicians can diagnose and fix problems more efficiently than general handymen. Their specialized knowledge ensures that repairs are done correctly the first time, preventing repeated issues.
- *Peace of Mind:* Knowing that you have a dependable technician available reduces stress and allows you to focus on other aspects of your business. Reliable support means you can operate with confidence, knowing that any issues will be promptly addressed.

Maintaining the Relationship

To ensure a lasting and productive partnership, it's important to maintain a positive relationship with your technicians. Here are some tips:

- *Timely Payments:* Ensure that you pay for services promptly according to your agreement. Reliable payment fosters goodwill and encourages technicians to prioritize your business.
- *Provide Feedback:* Offer constructive feedback on the services provided. Positive feedback reinforces good work, while constructive criticism helps improve service quality.
- *Show Appreciation:* Acknowledge and appreciate the efforts of your technicians. Simple gestures, such as thank-you notes or occasional bonuses, can strengthen your relationship and foster loyalty.

By building and maintaining strong partnerships with reliable repair technicians, you can ensure that your vending machines remain in excellent working condition. These partnerships minimize downtime, enhance machine reliability, and ultimately contribute to the success and profitability of your business.

Chapter 4
Location is Key: Mastering the Scouting Game

Success in the vending machine business hinges on one critical factor: location. Just like in real estate, where "location, location, location" is the mantra, the placement of your vending machines can make or break your business. High-traffic spots, where a steady stream of potential customers passes by, are the golden ticket to consistent sales and profitability.

Bustling office buildings, busy schools, thriving gyms, or crowded transportation hubs. These are the locations where people need quick, convenient access to snacks and drinks, making them the perfect spots for your machines. But finding and securing these prime locations requires more than just luck; it requires strategic planning, negotiation skills, and savvy marketing.

The first step in mastering the scouting game is thorough research. You need to understand the foot traffic patterns, customer demographics, and competitive landscape of potential locations. Visiting these sites at different times of the day will give you a realistic picture of peak periods and customer flow. It's essential to look beyond just the volume of foot traffic and consider who these people are and what products they are likely to purchase. Are they office workers in need of a mid-afternoon energy boost? Students looking for a quick snack between classes? Gym-goers wanting a post-workout protein bar?

Once you have identified potential high-traffic locations, the next challenge is negotiating placement. This is where your skills in persuasion and building relationships come into play. Property owners and managers need to see the value in having your vending machines on their premises. Highlighting the benefits, such as providing a convenient service for their tenants or customers and offering a share of the revenue, can make your proposal more attractive. Sometimes, offering a trial period can help demonstrate the benefits without requiring a long-term commitment upfront.

But securing a location is only part of the equation. You also need to make sure that people know where your machines are and are motivated to use them. This is where the power of social media comes into play. By promoting your vending machine locations on platforms like Instagram, Facebook, and Twitter, you can reach a wider audience and drive more traffic to your machines. Announce new locations with eye-catching photos and engaging posts. Partner with local businesses to cross-promote and create a buzz around your vending machines. Running social media contests and promotions can also generate excitement and encourage more people to seek out your machines.

High-Traffic Havens: Identifying Prime Locations

Understanding Location Factors

Foot Traffic

Foot traffic is the lifeblood of your vending machine business. The more people who pass by your machine, the higher your sales potential. Here's how to evaluate foot traffic effectively:

Start by observing potential locations at different times of the day and week. Look for consistent and substantial foot traffic, not just occasional spikes. High-traffic times, such as mornings, lunch hours, and evenings, are especially important.

Pay attention to the flow of people. Are they moving quickly through the area, or do they linger? Locations where people spend more time are generally better because customers are more likely to notice and use your vending machine.

For a more quantitative approach, count the number of people passing by during peak times over several days to establish an average. This data will help you compare potential locations objectively.

Be aware of any seasonal variations in foot traffic. For instance, schools may see a significant drop during summer vacations, while gyms might be busier in January due to New Year's resolutions.

Demographics

Knowing who your customers are is just as important as knowing how many there are. Different demographics have different needs and preferences, influencing your product offerings and marketing strategies.

Analyze the age and gender of people frequenting the area. Younger demographics might prefer trendy snacks and beverages, while older individuals might lean towards healthier options or items catering to specific dietary needs.

Consider the income level of the area, as it affects purchasing power. High-income areas might support premium pricing for high-quality or specialty products, whereas lower-income areas require competitive pricing.

Understand the daily routines and lifestyles of your potential customers. Office workers might appreciate coffee and quick snacks, students might look for energy drinks and affordable snacks, while gym-goers might seek protein bars and sports drinks.

Be mindful of cultural and social factors that may influence buying behavior. For example, areas with a high concentration of health-conscious individuals may have a higher demand for organic and non-GMO products.

Competition

Understanding the competitive landscape is essential to determine whether a location is viable and how to differentiate your offerings.

Look for other vending machines, convenience stores, and cafes nearby. Analyze their product offerings, prices, and customer base. Knowing what your competition is doing can help you identify market gaps.

Observe the success of nearby vending machines. Are they frequently used, or do they seem neglected? Successful competitors indicate strong demand, but you'll need to offer something unique to draw customers away.

Offer products that your competitors don't. If nearby vending machines stock traditional snacks, consider offering healthier alternatives, premium beverages, or specialty items.

Ensure your pricing is competitive. Conduct a price comparison with nearby vending machines and convenience stores to ensure you're offering good value. If you can't compete on price, focus on product quality and unique offerings.

Be cautious of oversaturation. If there are already many vending machines in a small area, it might be harder to attract customers. Look for locations where you can be the first or where there is room for one more without crowding the market.

Combining Factors for the Best Locations

Combine your analysis of foot traffic, demographics, and competition to identify the best locations for your vending machines. List potential locations, score each factor, and calculate totals to compare different spots objectively.

Consider pilot testing by placing a machine in a high-scoring location on a temporary basis. Monitor its performance closely to validate your analysis. Based on the pilot test and your overall evaluation, choose the best locations for your vending machines.

By thoroughly analyzing foot traffic, demographics, and competition, you can identify prime locations for your vending machines. Understanding these factors will help you make informed decisions, ensuring that your machines are placed where they are most likely to succeed. With the right locations, you can maximize sales, enhance customer satisfaction, and achieve sustained profitability in your vending machine business.

Negotiating Winning Deals

Highlight the Benefits

When approaching property owners or managers, emphasize the benefits that your vending machines will bring to their location. Focus on how your machines can enhance their offerings and provide added convenience to their visitors, employees, or customers. Key points to highlight include:

Convenience: Vending machines offer quick and easy access to snacks and beverages, which is especially valuable in busy locations where people may not have time to visit a store.

Added Amenities: Having vending machines on-site can be seen as an added amenity, enhancing the overall appeal of the location for tenants, employees, or customers.

Revenue Sharing: Propose a revenue-sharing model where the property owner receives a percentage of the profits. This financial incentive can make your proposal more attractive.

Minimal Effort: Explain that once the machine is installed, there is minimal effort required from the property owner, as you will handle all stocking and maintenance.

Propose a Trial Period

Offering a trial period can help property owners see the benefits of having your vending machines without making a long-term commitment upfront. A trial period allows them to evaluate the impact and convenience of the machines. Here's how to structure a trial period:

Set Clear Terms: Clearly outline the duration of the trial period (e.g., three months) and the terms, including maintenance and stocking responsibilities.

Performance Metrics: Agree on performance metrics to evaluate the trial, such as sales volume and customer feedback.

Post-Trial Options: Discuss what happens after the trial period. If the results are positive, propose transitioning to a longer-term agreement.

Be Flexible and Open to Negotiation

Flexibility can be a significant advantage in negotiations. Be open to discussing various terms and arrangements that can meet both your needs and those of the property owner. Key points to consider include:

Placement Fees vs. Revenue Sharing: Some property owners may prefer a flat placement fee instead of a revenue-sharing model. Be prepared to offer both options and discuss which works best for them.

Service Frequency: Negotiate the frequency of machine servicing and restocking to ensure it aligns with the property's schedule and needs.

Machine Type and Products: Tailor your machine types and product offerings to the specific location. For instance, a gym might prefer healthy snacks and protein drinks, while an office building might favor coffee and quick snacks.

Present a Professional Proposal

A well-prepared, professional proposal can make a strong impression and demonstrate your commitment and reliability. Your proposal should include:

Business Overview: Provide a brief overview of your vending machine business, including your experience, reputation, and track record.

Benefits Summary: Clearly outline the benefits of having your vending machines on their premises.

Proposed Terms: Detail the proposed terms of the agreement, including the type of machines, product offerings, revenue-sharing model or placement fees, and maintenance schedule.

References and Testimonials: Include references and testimonials from other locations where your machines have been successful. This adds credibility and reassures the property owner of your professionalism.

Build Relationships

Building strong relationships with property owners and managers can facilitate smoother negotiations and long-term success. Focus on establishing trust and demonstrating your commitment to providing excellent service. Tips for building relationships include:

Regular Communication: Keep open lines of communication before, during, and after negotiations. Regular updates and check-ins can help build a strong rapport.

Responsive Service: Be responsive to any concerns or issues that arise. Prompt and effective problem-solving shows that you are dependable.

Personal Touch: Whenever possible, meet property owners and managers in person. Face-to-face meetings can help establish a personal connection and build trust.

Address Concerns Proactively

Anticipate and address any concerns the property owner might have. Common concerns include potential noise, cleanliness, and maintenance issues. Provide reassurances and solutions, such as:

Noise: Explain that modern vending machines are designed to operate quietly.

Cleanliness: Commit to regular cleaning and maintenance to keep the area around the machine tidy.

Maintenance: Ensure them that you have a robust maintenance plan in place to address any issues promptly.

Effective negotiation not only helps you secure prime spots but also establishes a foundation for long-term partnerships and ongoing business growth.

Social Media Location Promotion

High-traffic spots such as gyms, co-working spaces, schools, and office buildings benefit greatly from an active and engaging social media presence. Here's how to effectively use social media to showcase your vending machine locations.

Create Engaging Content

Creating engaging content is key to attracting and retaining your audience. Start by announcing new locations with eye-catching posts that include high-quality photos of your vending machines and their surroundings. Highlight the convenience and variety of products available. Sharing behind-the-scenes content of stocking and maintaining the machines can add a personal touch to your business, showing the effort you put into keeping the machines well-stocked and clean.

Customer Spotlights

Customer spotlights are a powerful way to build trust and show-case satisfaction. Feature your customers using the vending machines and encourage them to share their experiences and tag your business in their posts. Regularly highlight the products available in your machines, sharing information about new items, popular snacks, or any special promotions. Use appealing visuals and descriptions to entice potential customers.

Leverage Partnerships

Collaborating with high-traffic location partners can amplify your reach and credibility. Work with gyms, co-working spaces, or other high-traffic locations to run joint promotions. Offer discounts to gym members who purchase from your vending machines, or collaborate on a social media giveaway. Partner with the businesses hosting your machines to cross-promote on social media. They can share your posts with their followers, and you can reciprocate, helping both parties reach a wider audience.

Organizing small events or pop-ups in collaboration with your location partners can generate buzz. For example, host a healthy snack tasting session at a gym or a coffee break event at a co-working space. Share these events live on social media to engage your audience in real-time.

Utilize Hashtags and Geotags

Maximizing the visibility of your posts involves using relevant hashtags and geotags. Use popular and relevant hashtags to increase the discoverability of your posts. Combine general vending machine hashtags with specific ones related to your location. Always geotag your posts with the specific location of your vending machines. This helps local customers find your machines more easily when they search for places nearby on social media platforms.

Run Contests and Promotions

Running contests and promotions is an excellent way to generate buzz and attract new customers. Encourage customers to take a photo with your vending machine and share it on social media with a specific hashtag. Offer a prize for the best photo or a random draw. This not only promotes your machines but also generates user-generated content. Share exclusive discount codes on social media that customers can use at specific vending machine locations. This drives traffic to your machines and incentivizes purchases. Promote limited-time offers or seasonal products on social media, creating urgency by emphasizing the time-sensitive nature of the promotion.

Engage With Your Audience

Building a loyal following on social media requires active engagement. Respond to comments, questions, and messages promptly, showing that you value feedback and are attentive to their needs. Thank customers for their positive feedback and address any concerns they may have. Highlighting positive interactions fosters a sense of community and trust. Use social media to solicit feedback on product preferences, new items, or potential improvements, engaging your audience while gaining valuable insights for your business.

Analyze and Refine Your Strategy

Regularly reviewing your social media analytics helps you understand what content resonates most with your audience and refine your strategy accordingly. Monitor likes, comments, shares, and overall engagement rates to identify which posts perform best and why. Use analytics tools to track how much traffic your social media efforts are driving to your vending machine locations, adjusting your strategy based on these insights to maximize impact. Pay attention to demographic data provided by social media platforms, tailoring your content and promotions more effectively.

Using social media to promote your vending machine locations is a powerful way to increase visibility and attract more customers. By creating engaging content, leveraging partnerships, utilizing hashtags and geotags, running contests and promotions, engaging with your audience, and analyzing your efforts, you can effectively showcase your high-traffic locations and drive business growth. This strategic approach not only boosts sales but also builds a loyal customer base, ensuring long-term success for your vending machine business.

Building Location Partnerships

Identifying Potential Partners:

Offices

Offices are ideal for vending machines because they house many employees who need convenient access to snacks and beverages throughout the day. Office buildings, especially those with multiple companies or large corporations, have high foot traffic. Employees, visitors, and maintenance staff create a constant stream of potential customers. Employees often have limited time for breaks and lunch, making convenient access to snacks and drinks highly desirable. Vending machines provide quick and easy options without leaving the premises. Office workers have varied snack preferences, from quick energy boosts to healthier options. Stocking a mix of traditional snacks, healthy alternatives, and beverages caters to this diverse audience.

To approach office buildings, start by identifying office buildings and business parks in your target area. Focus on locations with a high density of companies and employees. Reach out to property managers or building administrators to discuss the benefits of having vending machines on-site. Highlight the convenience for employees and potential revenue-sharing opportunities. Customize your proposal to address the specific needs of the office environment. Offer a variety of products, including healthy snacks, and propose regular maintenance and restocking schedules.

Schools

Schools are another excellent location for vending machines. Students, teachers, and staff members benefit from the convenience of easily accessible snacks and beverages. Schools have a constant flow of students and staff who need snacks and drinks throughout the day. Break times, lunch periods, and after-school activities provide multiple opportunities for sales. Many schools are moving towards healthier snack options. Stocking nutritious snacks and drinks can meet the demand for healthier choices and comply with school policies. Schools often welcome partnerships that enhance student life and provide additional amenities. Vending machines can contribute to this by offering convenient and healthy snack options.

To approach schools, identify schools in your target area, focusing on high schools, colleges, and universities. Consider both public and private institutions. Reach out to school principals, administrators, or facility managers to discuss the benefits of vending machines. Highlight how your machines can provide convenient and healthy snack options for students and staff. Emphasize your commitment to offering healthy snacks that comply with school nutrition standards. Propose a variety of products that cater to the needs of students and staff.

Hospitals

Hospitals are high-traffic locations with a diverse group of people, including patients, visitors, and healthcare workers, all of whom need access to convenient food and drink options. Hospitals operate around the clock, providing a steady flow of potential customers at all hours. This constant demand makes vending machines a valuable addition to hospital amenities. Hospitals cater to a wide range of people, including patients, visitors, and staff. This diversity creates demand for a variety of products, from quick snacks to healthy meals. Healthcare workers often have limited time for breaks. Vending machines offer a quick and convenient way for staff to grab a snack or drink without leaving the hospital.

To approach hospitals, identify hospitals and healthcare facilities in your target area. Consider large hospitals, medical centers, and specialized clinics. Reach out to hospital administrators or facility managers to discuss the benefits of vending machines. Highlight the convenience for staff, patients, and visitors, and the potential for a revenue-sharing agreement. Propose a range of products that cater to the needs of a hospital environment. Include healthy snacks, quick meals, and beverages. Emphasize regular maintenance and restocking to ensure machines are always ready to serve.

Building Strong Partnerships

Building strong, lasting partnerships with these locations requires clear communication, reliability, and mutual benefits. Maintain open lines of communication with your partners. Regular updates and prompt responses to any issues build trust and demonstrate your commitment to providing excellent service. Ensure that your machines are well-maintained and consistently stocked. Reliable service is crucial to maintaining a positive relationship with your partners. Highlight the mutual benefits of the partnership. For example, offer revenue-sharing opportunities or contribute to the community by providing healthy snack options. Schedule regular reviews with your partners to discuss performance, address any concerns, and explore opportunities for improvement or expansion.

These locations offer high foot traffic and diverse customer needs, making them ideal for vending machines. By approaching potential partners with tailored proposals, emphasizing the benefits, and maintaining clear communication and reliability, you can establish successful partnerships that drive growth and profitability for your vending machine business.

Negotiating Mutually Beneficial Agreements

Understanding the Benefits

Before entering negotiations, it's important to understand and articulate the benefits for both parties. Vending machines provide added convenience for employees, students, patients, and visitors, enhancing the amenities of the location. For your business, prime locations translate into higher sales and increased revenue. By sharing this revenue with your partners, you create a win-win situation.

Research and Preparation

Effective negotiation begins with thorough research and preparation. Understand the needs and priorities of your potential partners. For offices, convenience and employee satisfaction are key. Schools might prioritize healthy snack options and compliance with nutrition guidelines. Hospitals will value around-the-clock availability and a variety of products to meet diverse needs.

Gather data on typical revenue generated by vending machines in similar locations. This will help you propose realistic and attractive revenue-sharing terms. Being well-prepared demonstrates professionalism and builds trust with your partners.

Propose Clear and Transparent Terms

When structuring a revenue-sharing agreement, clarity and transparency are essential. Here are the key components to include in your proposal:

Revenue Split: Clearly define how the revenue will be divided between your business and the partner location. Common splits range from 10% to 25% of gross sales going to the location. The exact percentage can vary based on factors such as foot traffic, machine type, and product offerings.

Payment Schedule: Specify how and when payments will be made. Monthly payments are standard, but you can adjust this based on the partner's preferences. Include details on how sales will be tracked and reported to ensure transparency.

Product Selection: Outline the types of products that will be stocked in the machines. For schools and hospitals, emphasize healthy and compliant options. For offices, include a mix of snacks and beverages that cater to diverse preferences.

Maintenance and Restocking: Detail the responsibilities for maintaining and restocking the machines. Ensure that your partners understand you will handle all operational aspects, minimizing their involvement and ensuring consistent service.

Trial Period: Offer a trial period to allow partners to assess the benefits without a long-term commitment. A three to six-month trial period can demonstrate the positive impact of the vending machines and pave the way for a longer-term agreement.

Negotiation Strategies

Emphasize Mutual Benefits: Highlight how the vending machines will enhance the location's amenities, improve convenience, and potentially generate additional income. Emphasize that a revenue-sharing agreement aligns both parties' interests in maximizing sales.

Be Flexible: Be prepared to adjust your proposal based on the partner's feedback. Flexibility can help you reach a mutually beneficial agreement. For example, you might offer a higher revenue share for locations with exceptionally high foot traffic or agree to stock specific product types requested by the partner.

Build Trust: Establish trust by being transparent about costs, potential revenue, and the benefits of the partnership. Share testimonials or case studies from other successful partnerships to demonstrate your reliability and the value you bring.

Address Concerns: Proactively address any concerns the partner might have. Common concerns include noise, cleanliness, and maintenance. Reassure partners by explaining your maintenance schedules, cleaning procedures, and commitment to quick repairs.

Drafting the Agreement

Once terms are agreed upon, formalize the arrangement in a written agreement. This document should clearly outline all terms discussed, including the revenue split, payment schedule, product selection, maintenance responsibilities, and trial period. Ensure both parties review and sign the agreement to formalize the partnership.

Monitoring and Communication

Maintaining a successful partnership requires ongoing communication and monitoring. Regularly review sales data, share reports with your partners, and ensure timely payments. Schedule periodic check-ins to address any concerns, discuss performance, and explore opportunities for improvement or expansion.

Adjusting Terms

As the partnership progresses, be open to adjusting terms if necessary. For example, if sales exceed expectations, you might renegotiate the revenue share to reflect the increased success. Conversely, if sales are lower than anticipated, explore ways to boost performance or adjust the agreement to ensure sustainability for both parties..

Maintaining Positive Relationships

Clear and Consistent Communication

Effective communication is the foundation of any strong partnership. Regularly update location owners on important matters related to your vending machines. Provide monthly or quarterly performance reports detailing sales, popular products, and any issues encountered. Inform owners about scheduled maintenance visits to avoid surprises and reassure them that the machines are well cared for. Establish a clear channel for feedback and encourage location owners to share their concerns or suggestions, responding promptly to their inquiries.

Reliability and Professionalism

Being reliable and professional in all interactions strengthens your credibility and fosters trust. Ensure that any revenue-sharing payments are made on time and accurately. Stick to agreed-upon schedules for restocking and maintenance, showing respect for the location owner's time and commitment to keeping the machines operational. Maintain a professional demeanor in all interactions, whether in person, via email, or over the phone.

Demonstrate Value

Show location owners that having your vending machines on their premises is beneficial. Emphasize how the machines provide convenience to employees, students, patients, or visitors, enhancing the overall experience at the location. Regularly update owners on the financial benefits, such as shared revenue, and how it positively contributes to their operations. Tailor the product selection to meet the specific needs and preferences of the location's users and regularly review and adjust the offerings based on sales data and feedback.

Flexibility and Adaptability

Being flexible and willing to adapt to changing circumstances or needs can strengthen partnerships. Customize your offerings to meet the unique needs of each location, improving satisfaction and sales. Address any problems or complaints swiftly and efficiently, demonstrating your capability in handling issues professionally. If circumstances change, such as a significant increase

in foot traffic or a new competitor in the area, be willing to renegotiate terms to ensure both parties continue to benefit.

Regular Check-Ins

Scheduling regular check-ins with location owners helps maintain strong relationships. These meetings can be formal or infor-
mal, but their purpose is to discuss performance, seek feedback,
and plan for the future. Actively seek feedback on how the partnership is going and any potential changes that could enhance it.
Discuss future plans, such as adding more machines, introducing
new products, or participating in joint promotions.

Show Appreciation

Expressing appreciation for the partnership can go a long way in
maintaining positive relationships. Send occasional thank you
notes or emails expressing gratitude for their partnership and
support. Acknowledge holidays or special occasions with a
greeting card or a small token of appreciation. Publicly acknowledge their support in any promotional materials or social media
posts, with their permission.

Community Engagement

Engaging with the community can strengthen your relationship
with location owners, especially in schools and hospitals.
Consider participating in or sponsoring community events,
contributing to local causes, or collaborating on community
initiatives. Demonstrating that your business is committed to the
well-being of the community can enhance your reputation and
deepen your partnership.

Continuous Improvement

Always strive to improve the service you provide. Regularly
review your operations, seek out new technologies or practices

that can enhance efficiency, and keep up with industry trends. Showing a commitment to continuous improvement reflects well on your professionalism and dedication to the partnership.

Chapter 5
Product Mix Formula: Crafting the Perfect Sales Potion

The secret to a successful vending machine business lies in the perfect product mix. Just like a master chef crafts a dish by combining the right ingredients, your vending machines need a carefully curated selection of products to maximize sales and customer satisfaction. It's not just about stocking your machines with random snacks and drinks; it's about understanding your customers' preferences, staying ahead of market trends, and offering a variety that caters to diverse tastes and needs.

Whether it's the student rushing between classes, the office worker craving an afternoon pick-me-up, or the gym-goer looking for a post-workout snack, your goal is to meet their needs with the right products. This chapter will guide you through the art and science of crafting the perfect sales potion – a product mix that not only attracts customers but also keeps them coming back for more.

Decoding Customer Preferences

Conducting Market Research

Surveying Target Demographics

Gathering detailed information about your target demographics is the first step. This involves understanding who your customers are, their needs, and their buying behaviors. Direct surveys are an effective method for collecting this data. Create engaging surveys to distribute via email, social media, or QR codes displayed on your vending machines. Ask questions about favorite snacks, beverages, and any new products they'd like to see. Offering a small incentive, such as a discount or a free item, can increase participation rates.

Focus group sessions with a diverse group of people who frequent your vending machine locations can provide deeper insights. These sessions allow for in-depth discussions about product preferences and can reveal details that surveys might miss. Focus groups also enable follow-up questions and clarification of responses, leading to more comprehensive feedback.

Observation is another practical approach. Spend time watching customer behavior at your vending machines. Note which products are purchased frequently and which are often overlooked. Pay attention to the times of day when different products are popular. This hands-on approach offers real-time insights into customer preferences.

Install a feedback system on your vending machines, such as a suggestion box or a digital feedback option. Encourage customers to leave comments about their experiences and product preferences. This ongoing feedback helps you stay attuned to changing tastes and needs.

Analyzing Sales Data

Once you have gathered survey data, analyze sales data from your vending machines. This quantitative data shows what products are actually being purchased and highlights trends and patterns. Generate regular sales reports from your vending machine management software. These reports should include data on product sales volumes, revenue, and inventory turnover. Analyzing these reports helps identify best-sellers and slow-moving items.

Evaluate the performance of each product. Look for patterns like seasonal variations in sales or spikes in demand during specific times of the day. Understanding these patterns allows you to adjust your inventory to meet customer demand.

Segment your customer base based on demographics such as age, gender, location, and purchasing behavior. This segmentation helps tailor your product offerings to different customer groups. For example, students may prefer affordable, high-energy snacks, while office workers might opt for healthier options and premium coffee.

Keep an eye on broader market trends that may influence customer preferences. For instance, the growing demand for plant-based snacks, organic products, and low-sugar beverages can guide your product selection. Comparing your sales data with these trends helps stay ahead of the curve and meet emerging customer needs.

Implementing Insights

After gathering and analyzing customer data, implement the insights to optimize your product mix. Ensure your vending machines are consistently stocked with the most popular products identified through your research. Prioritize high-demand items to prevent stockouts and maximize sales.

Introduce new products based on customer feedback and market trends. Conduct limited-time trials of new items to gauge customer response before making them a permanent part of your inventory.

Tailor the product mix for different locations based on the specific preferences of each customer base. For example, a vending machine in a gym might stock protein bars and sports drinks, while one in an office building might offer gourmet snacks and premium coffee.

Continuously monitor sales data and customer feedback to ensure your product mix remains relevant. Be prepared to adjust as customer preferences evolve and new trends emerge.

Use promotions and discounts to boost sales of new or less popular products. Special offers can encourage customers to try new items and provide valuable data on their potential long-term success.

Staying on Top of Trends

With constantly changing consumer preferences, it's essential to identify the latest snack options and trends. Social media listening is a powerful tool that can help you stay ahead of the curve by tracking what people are talking about, liking, and sharing. Here's how to effectively use social media listening to identify emerging snack options and customer preferences.

Understanding Social Media Listening

Social media listening involves monitoring various social media platforms to gather information about customer preferences, emerging trends, and market insights. Unlike social media monitoring, which focuses on tracking specific metrics like mentions and engagement, social media listening goes deeper. It analyzes the broader conversations happening online to identify patterns and trends that can inform your vending machine product strategy.

Choosing the Right Tools

There are several tools available for social media listening, each offering different features. Some popular tools include Hootsuite, Brandwatch, Sprout Social, and Mention. These tools can help you track keywords, hashtags, and trends relevant to your business. Choose a tool that fits your needs and budget, and make sure it can monitor multiple platforms, including Facebook, Twitter, Instagram, and Reddit.

Tracking Relevant Keywords and Hashtags

To identify emerging snack options and customer preferences, start by tracking relevant keywords and hashtags. These could include terms like #snacks, #healthysnacks, #vegan, #glutenfree, #organic, and #proteinbars. By monitoring these keywords and hashtags, you can see what types of snacks are currently popular and what people are saying about them. Pay attention to both positive and negative comments to understand customer sentiments and preferences.

Analyzing Conversations and Engagement

Once you have your keywords and hashtags set up, analyze the conversations and engagement around them. Look at the number of mentions, likes, shares, and comments each post receives. High engagement levels often indicate popular trends and products. Additionally, look at the context of these conversations. Are people discussing these snacks in a positive or negative light? What specific features or benefits are they highlighting? This analysis can provide deeper insights into what customers value in their snack choices.

Identifying Influencers and Trendsetters

Influencers and trendsetters play a significant role in shaping consumer preferences. Identify key influencers in the snack and vending machine space who have a large following and high engagement rates. Follow these influencers to see what products they are promoting and what trends they are talking about. Often, influencers are early adopters of new trends, giving you a heads-up on what might become popular next.

Spotting Emerging Trends

Social media listening can help you spot emerging trends before they become mainstream. For example, if you notice a sudden increase in conversations around plant-based snacks or keto-friendly products, it might indicate a growing trend. Similarly, if a new type of snack, like seaweed chips or cricket protein bars, starts gaining traction, it's worth considering for your vending machines. Staying agile and ready to adapt to these trends can keep your product offerings fresh and appealing.

Engaging With Your Audience

Social media listening isn't just about gathering information; it's also about engaging with your audience. Respond to comments and questions about your products, and participate in conversations about trending snacks. Engaging with your audience can provide direct feedback and build stronger customer relationships. It also demonstrates that you are attentive and responsive to customer preferences, which can enhance your brand reputation.

Using Insights to Inform Product Selection

The insights gained from social media listening should directly inform your product selection strategy. For example, if you notice a growing demand for vegan snacks, start incorporating more vegan options into your vending machines. If gluten-free products are trending, ensure you have a variety of gluten-free snacks available. Continuously update your product mix based on the latest trends to meet customer expectations and stay competitive.

Monitoring Competitors

Social media listening also allows you to keep an eye on your competitors. Track what other vending machine businesses are doing, what products they are promoting, and how customers are responding. This competitive analysis can reveal gaps in the market that you can exploit or highlight areas where you can differentiate your offerings.

Regularly Reviewing and Adapting

Trends can change quickly, so it's important to regularly review your social media listening data and adapt your strategies accordingly. Set up regular intervals for analyzing your data—monthly or quarterly—and adjust your product offerings based on the latest insights. Staying proactive and responsive to changes in consumer preferences will help you maintain a compctitive edge.

Utilizing Social Media for Customer Feedback

Choosing the Right Platforms

The first step is to choose the right social media platforms for engaging with your audience. Facebook, Instagram, Twitter, and LinkedIn are all excellent options, each offering unique features for running polls and gathering feedback. Facebook and Instagram, for example, have built-in polling features in their Stories, making it easy to ask questions and get quick responses. Twitter's poll feature is also straightforward and allows for real-time interaction. LinkedIn can be particularly useful for engaging with a professional audience, such as those who might frequent vending machines in office buildings.

Creating Engaging Polls

To get meaningful feedback, it's crucial to create engaging and relevant polls. Here's how to design effective polls:

Keep It Simple: Ask clear, concise questions that are easy to understand. Avoid complex or multi-part questions that might confuse respondents.

Be Specific: Focus on specific products or categories to get targeted feedback. For example, ask, "Which type of snack would you like to see in our vending machines?" with options like chips, nuts, or granola bars.

Use Visuals: Incorporate images or videos to make the polls more engaging. Visuals can help respondents better understand the choices and feel more connected to the poll.

Limit Options: Provide a manageable number of options to avoid overwhelming respondents. Typically, 3-5 choices work best.

Encourage Participation: Promote your polls by sharing them across your social media channels and encouraging followers to participate. You can also incentivize participation with small rewards, such as a discount code or entry into a giveaway.

Gathering Feedback

In addition to running polls, actively gathering feedback through social media is essential. Here are some strategies to consider:

Ask Open-Ended Questions: Use your social media posts to ask open-ended questions about product preferences and suggestions. For example, "What new snacks would you like to see in our vending machines?" encourages followers to share their thoughts in the comments.

Monitor Comments and Messages: Pay close attention to comments and direct messages from your followers. This feedback can provide insights into customer preferences and high-light any issues or suggestions they might have.

Conduct Surveys: Use social media to promote more detailed surveys hosted on platforms like SurveyMonkey or Google Forms. These surveys can delve deeper into customer preferences and gather more comprehensive data.

Engage With Followers: Respond to comments and messages promptly, showing that you value their input. Engaging with your audience builds trust and encourages more feedback.

Analyzing Feedback

Once you've gathered feedback, it's crucial to analyze the data to identify trends and actionable insights. Here's how to effectively analyze customer feedback:

Categorize Responses: Group feedback into categories such as product preferences, new product suggestions, and general comments. This helps identify common themes and trends.

Quantify Poll Results: Summarize poll results in percentages or charts to easily visualize preferences. For example, if 60% of respondents prefer healthy snacks, this indicates a strong demand for such products.

Identify Common Suggestions: Look for recurring suggestions or comments. If multiple customers request a specific product or improvement, it's a strong indicator of demand.

Consider Sentiment: Pay attention to the tone of the feedback. Positive feedback highlights what's working well, while negative feedback can indicate areas for improvement.

Implementing Changes

Use the insights gained from customer feedback to make

informed decisions about your product selection. Here's how to implement changes based on feedback:

Introduce Popular Products: Add the most requested products to your vending machines. If a particular snack or drink is frequently mentioned, prioritize its inclusion.

Rotate Stock: Regularly update and rotate your product offerings based on feedback and sales data. This keeps your vending machines fresh and appealing to repeat customers.

Promote New Additions: Use social media to announce new products and changes based on customer feedback. Highlighting that you've listened to and acted on their suggestions can strengthen customer loyalty.

Monitor Results: After implementing changes, continue to monitor sales and gather feedback to ensure the new products meet customer expectations. This ongoing process helps fine-tune your product mix and keeps your offerings aligned with customer preferences.

Building a Community

Engaging with customers on social media goes beyond just gathering feedback; it's about building a community. Here's how to foster a sense of community among your followers:

Share User-Generated Content: Encourage customers to share photos of their purchases from your vending machines and feature this content on your social media pages.

Host Contests and Giveaways: Run contests and giveaways to engage your audience and gather more feedback. For example, ask followers to suggest a new product for a chance to win a prize.

Provide Updates: Keep your audience informed about any

changes or new additions to your vending machines. Regular updates show that you're active and responsive to their needs.

Building a Balanced Inventory

Analyzing Product Profit Margins

This balance involves prioritizing high-profit items while also ensuring customer favorites are always available. By analyzing product profit margins and understanding customer preferences, you can optimize your inventory to maximize profits and keep customers satisfied. Here's how to achieve this balance effectively.

Understanding Product Profit Margins

Product profit margin is the difference between the cost of acquiring a product and the revenue generated from selling it. Higher profit margins mean more earnings per unit sold. To analyze product profit margins, you need to calculate the cost of each item, including purchase price, shipping, and any additional costs. Subtract this total cost from the selling price to determine the profit margin. Products with higher margins contribute more significantly to your overall profitability, so identifying these items is the first step.

Collecting and Analyzing Sales Data

Collecting and analyzing sales data from your vending machines is essential. Use vending machine management software to track sales volumes, revenue, and profit margins for each product. This data helps identify which items are high-profit and which are customer favorites. Look for trends in your sales data, such as seasonal spikes in demand for certain products or consistent best-sellers. This information will guide your inventory decisions.

Prioritizing High-Profit Items

Once you've identified high-profit items, prioritize stocking these products to maximize your revenue. However, it's important not to fill your vending machines solely with high-margin items. Customers have diverse preferences, and focusing only on high-profit items can lead to dissatisfaction and decreased sales. Instead, find a balance by mixing high-profit items with customer favorites.

Maintaining Customer Favorites

Customer favorites are the products that sell consistently well, regardless of their profit margins. These items keep customers returning to your vending machines, providing a steady revenue stream. While some customer favorites might have lower profit margins, their high turnover rate can still make them valuable. Maintain a balance by ensuring these popular items are always available, alongside your high-profit items.

Diversifying Your Product Mix

A diverse product mix caters to a wider audience, increasing the likelihood of attracting more customers. Include a variety of snacks, beverages, and healthier options to meet different preferences and dietary needs. For example, include traditional snacks like chips and candy, as well as healthier options like nuts, granola bars, and bottled water. This diversity not only satisfies a broader customer base but also encourages impulse purchases.

Seasonal Adjustments

Adjust your inventory seasonally to capitalize on changing customer preferences. During colder months, hot beverages and comfort foods may be more popular, while refreshing drinks and lighter snacks might sell better in warmer months. Monitor seasonal trends in your sales data and adjust your inventory accordingly to maximize sales.

Product Placement and Visibility

The placement of products within your vending machines can influence sales. Position high-profit items and customer favorites at eye level or in easily accessible spots. Products that are prominently displayed are more likely to be noticed and purchased. Additionally, grouping similar items together can help customers find what they're looking for more easily, enhancing their overall experience.

Promotions and Discounts

Running promotions and offering discounts on certain products can help manage inventory and boost sales. For example, bundle high-profit items with lower-margin favorites to encourage customers to buy more. Limited-time offers or discounts on slow-moving items can also help clear out inventory and make room for new products.

Regular Inventory Reviews

Conduct regular inventory reviews to ensure your product mix remains balanced and relevant. This involves analyzing sales data, monitoring customer feedback, and staying informed about market trends. Regular reviews help you identify underperforming items that can be replaced with higher-demand products, ensuring your inventory stays fresh and appealing.

Supplier Relationships

Building strong relationships with suppliers can help you negotiate better prices and secure high-quality products. Reliable suppliers can also provide insights into new and trending products, helping you stay ahead of the competition. Regularly review your supplier agreements to ensure you're getting the best possible prices and terms.

Continuous Improvement

Continuously improving your inventory management practices is key to long-term success. Stay informed about industry best practices, attend trade shows, and network with other vending machine operators to learn new strategies. Implementing new ideas and technologies can help you optimize your inventory and increase profitability.

Considering Seasonality and Location

Different times of the year and various locations bring unique customer preferences and demands. By understanding these factors, you can tailor your product offerings to meet changing needs and maximize profitability. Here's how to effectively adapt your product selection based on seasonal trends and specific location demographics.

Understanding Seasonal Trends

Seasonal trends significantly impact consumer preferences. As the seasons change, so do the types of products customers crave. For instance, during the summer, people tend to prefer cold beverages, ice cream, and lighter snacks. In contrast, winter months often see a rise in demand for hot drinks, comfort foods, and heartier snacks. To capitalize on these trends, it's essential to adjust your product mix accordingly.

Start by analyzing sales data from previous years to identify seasonal patterns. Look for trends in product popularity during different times of the year. This historical data can provide valuable insights into which products to stock more heavily during specific seasons. Additionally, consider incorporating seasonal products that cater to holiday periods, such as special treats during Christmas or Halloween-themed snacks in October.

Adapting Product Selection

To effectively adapt your product selection, consider the following strategies:

Regularly Review Sales Data: Continuously monitor and analyze sales data to identify trends and preferences at each location. Use this information to adjust your inventory based on what is selling well and what isn't. Regular reviews help you stay responsive to changing customer needs and preferences.

Engage With Customers: Use social media and feedback mechanisms to engage with your customers and gather insights into their preferences. Running polls, asking for suggestions, and reading comments can provide valuable feedback on what products to stock and when to make changes.

Test and Rotate Products: Regularly introduce new products and rotate your inventory to keep it fresh and appealing. Conduct limited-time trials of new items to gauge customer interest before making them a permanent part of your inventory. This strategy allows you to stay current with trends and continuously offer something new to your customers.

Seasonal Promotions: Run seasonal promotions and discounts to highlight specific products that align with the time of year. For example, offer discounts on cold beverages and ice cream during the summer or promote hot drinks and comfort foods in the winter. Seasonal promotions can boost sales and attract more customers to your vending machines.

Tailor Product Mix by Location: Customize the product mix for each vending machine based on its specific location. Use demographic data and customer feedback to determine the most popular products for each audience. This tailored approach ensures that your vending machines meet the unique needs of each location's customer base.

Stay Informed on Trends: Keep up-to-date with industry trends and emerging products by attending trade shows, reading industry publications, and networking with other vending machine operators. Staying informed about new products and market trends allows you to quickly adapt and incorporate popular items into your inventory.

Offering Healthy Options and Catering to Dietary Needs

As more people become health-conscious and aware of their dietary restrictions, providing a variety of healthy snacks and products that cater to specific dietary needs is essential. Here's how to effectively offer healthy options and cater to dietary restrictions in your vending machines.

Understanding the Demand for Healthy Snacks

Consumers are increasingly seeking snacks that provide nutritional value without compromising on taste. By offering a range of healthy options, you can attract a broader customer base, including those who might otherwise avoid vending machines due to a lack of nutritious choices.

Start by identifying popular healthy snacks that are both appealing and nutritious. Examples include:

Nuts and Seeds: Almonds, cashews, sunflower seeds, and mixed nuts are high in protein and healthy fats.

Dried Fruits: Dried apricots, raisins, and cranberries offer natural sweetness and fiber.

Whole Grain Snacks: Popcorn, whole grain crackers, and granola bars provide complex carbohydrates and fiber.

Protein Bars: These are popular among fitness enthusiasts and those looking for a quick energy boost.

Low-Sugar Options: Snacks with reduced sugar content, such as dark chocolate, are becoming increasingly popular.

Catering to Dietary Restrictions

Catering to dietary restrictions is crucial for meeting the needs of a diverse customer base. Common dietary restrictions include gluten-free, vegan, keto, and nut-free diets. By offering products that cater to these restrictions, you can ensure that everyone can find something suitable in your vending machines.

For gluten-free options, offer snacks such as rice cakes, gluten-free granola bars, and gluten-free crackers. Clearly label these items to make it easy for customers to identify them.

For vegan options, include plant-based snacks like vegetable chips, hummus and crackers, and vegan protein bars. Vegan snacks appeal not only to vegans but also to those looking for plant-based options.

For keto-friendly options, stock snacks that are low in carbs and high in healthy fats, such as cheese crisps, beef jerky, and keto bars. These options cater to customers following a ketogenic diet.

For nut-free options, ensure you have snacks that are safe for those with nut allergies, such as seed-based bars, fruit snacks, and certain popcorn varieties. Clearly label these items to avoid confusion.

Product Selection and Labeling

When selecting products, prioritize quality and transparency. Choose reputable brands known for their healthy and diet-friendly options. Ensure that all products are clearly labeled with their nutritional information and any relevant dietary certifications, such as gluten-free, vegan, or non-GMO.

Customer Feedback and Engagement

Engage with your customers to understand their preferences and needs better. Use social media and feedback mechanisms to ask for suggestions on healthy snacks and dietary-friendly options they'd like to see in your vending machines. This feedback can help you refine your product selection and ensure it aligns with customer demands.

Promotions and Education

Promote your healthy and dietary-friendly options to attract health-conscious customers. Use social media, signage on your vending machines, and promotional materials to highlight these products. Educate your customers about the benefits of healthy snacking and how your vending machines cater to various dietary needs. Sharing nutritional information and health benefits can encourage more customers to choose these options.

Regular Inventory Reviews

Regularly review your inventory to ensure that healthy and dietary-friendly options are well-stocked and fresh. Monitor sales data to identify popular items and adjust your product mix accordingly. If certain products are not performing well, replace them with new options based on customer feedback and market trends.

Chapter 6
Marketing Mastery: Leveraging Social Media and Beyond

In today's digital landscape, mastering marketing is not just about having a good product—it's about making sure people know about it, talk about it, and choose it over the competition. For vending machine businesses, this means utilizing every tool at your disposal to capture attention, engage customers, and build a loyal following. Welcome to "Marketing Mastery: Leveraging Social Media and Beyond," where we'll explore how to turn your vending machine business into a well-known and loved brand.

Think about the last time you discovered a new favorite snack. Chances are, you heard about it through social media, a friend's recommendation, or a catchy ad that made you curious enough to give it a try. This is the power of effective marketing: creating a buzz that leads to genuine interest and repeat purchases. In this chapter, we will dive deep into the strategies and tactics that can help you harness this power for your vending machines.

Social media platforms like Instagram, Facebook, Twitter, and TikTok are not just for personal use—they are powerful business tools that can help you connect with your audience in real-time.

By sharing engaging content, running interactive campaigns, and responding to customer feedback, you can build a community around your brand. Imagine your vending machines not just as sources of snacks, but as hubs of excitement where customers are eager to see what's new and share their experiences online.

Beyond social media, there are traditional marketing methods that should not be overlooked. Local advertising, partnerships with businesses and schools, and eye-catching machine designs can all play a significant role in increasing your visibility. Combining these with a strong social media presence creates a multifaceted marketing strategy that reaches customers wherever they are.

One of the most effective ways to market your vending machines is by telling a story. Share the journey of your business, highlight the uniqueness of your products, and showcase customer stories. People love to feel connected to the brands they support, and a compelling narrative can transform your vending machines from mere convenience into beloved fixtures in their daily lives.

Building Your Brand Online

Crafting a Compelling Social Media Presence

Social media platforms like Facebook and Instagram offer unparalleled opportunities to showcase your products, engage with customers, and build a recognizable brand. Here's how to create engaging profiles that highlight your vending machines and their locations effectively.

Choosing the Right Platforms

Selecting the right social media platforms is the first step in building your online presence. Facebook and Instagram are particularly effective for visual content and community engagement.

Facebook: Ideal for sharing detailed posts, updates, events, and engaging with a wide demographic.

Instagram: Perfect for visually-driven content, Instagram allows you to share high-quality images and videos of your vending machines, products, and locations.

Creating Engaging Profiles

Your social media profiles are the face of your brand online. Ensure they are complete, professional, and reflective of your brand's personality.

Profile Picture: Use a high-resolution image of your logo. This helps in building brand recognition.

Bio: Craft a concise and engaging bio that describes your business. Include relevant keywords and a call-to-action, such as a link to your website or a special promotion.

Showcasing Products and Locations

Visual content is key to capturing attention on social media. Regularly post high-quality photos and videos that showcase your vending machines, the products they offer, and their locations.

Product Photos: Highlight the variety of snacks and beverages available in your machines. Use well-lit, high-resolution images that make the products look appealing.

Location Shots: Show your vending machines in different locations. This not only highlights their accessibility but also promotes the places where they are located, such as gyms, schools, and office buildings.

Behind-the-Scenes: Share behind-the-scenes content of stocking and maintaining your vending machines. This adds a personal touch and builds trust with your audience.

Content Strategy

Developing a consistent content strategy helps keep your audience engaged and informed.

Posting Schedule: Establish a regular posting schedule to keep your audience engaged. Consistency is key to maintaining interest.

Content Mix: Use a mix of content types, including product highlights, customer testimonials, behind-the-scenes looks, and educational posts about healthy snacking or sustainability.

Interactive Posts: Encourage interaction through polls, questions, and contests. For example, ask followers to vote on new product additions or share their favorite snacks.

Engagement and Community Building

Engaging with your audience is crucial for building a loyal community around your brand.

Respond Promptly: Reply to comments and messages promptly. This shows that you value your followers' input and are attentive to their needs.

User-Generated Content: Encourage customers to share their experiences with your vending machines. Repost user-generated content to build a sense of community and authenticity.

Contests and Giveaways: Run contests and giveaways to boost engagement and attract new followers. Simple contests like "Share your favorite snack from our vending machine" can drive significant interaction.

Analytics and Adjustments

Monitoring your social media performance helps you understand what works and where improvements are needed.

Track Metrics: Use platform analytics to track metrics like engagement rates, follower growth, and post performance. This data provides insights into what types of content resonate most with your audience.

Adjust Strategy: Based on your analytics, adjust your content strategy to better meet the preferences of your audience. If product photos receive more engagement, focus more on show-casing different products.

Promotions and Advertising

Leverage the advertising tools available on social media platforms to reach a broader audience.

Targeted Ads: Use Facebook and Instagram ads to target specific demographics based on location, interests, and behaviors. This can help drive traffic to your vending machines, especially for new or underperforming locations.

Promotions: Offer exclusive promotions or discounts to your social media followers. This not only rewards your existing audience but also attracts new followers.

Collaborations and Partnerships

Collaborating with influencers and other brands can expand your reach and credibility.

Influencer Partnerships: Partner with local influencers who align with your brand. They can promote your vending machines and products to their followers, providing social proof and increasing visibility.

Cross-Promotions: Collaborate with businesses where your

vending machines are located. For instance, run a joint promotion with a gym or office building to attract their clientele.

Crafting a compelling social media presence is an ongoing process that involves showcasing your products and locations, engaging with your audience, and continuously refining your strategy

Content is King

High-Quality Photos

High-quality, visually appealing product photos are the cornerstone of any successful social media strategy. These images not only showcase what your vending machines offer but also highlight the quality and variety of the products. To capture the best product photos, use natural lighting whenever possible and ensure the images are clear and well-composed. Show different angles and close-ups to emphasize the texture and appeal of the snacks and beverages. Posting regularly about new and popular items keeps your audience informed and excited about what they can find in your vending machines. Consistent updates about the availability of seasonal or limited-time products can also drive interest and sales.

Location Announcements

Location announcements are another vital element of your content strategy. Whenever you install a new vending machine or move an existing one to a high-traffic area, share this news with your followers. This not only informs potential customers about where they can find your machines but also demonstrates the growth and reach of your business. Include photos of the new locations and highlight any unique features of the area, such as its convenience or the types of clientele it attracts. By tagging the location and using relevant hashtags, you can increase the visibility of these posts and attract local audiences who might not yet be aware of your services.

Behind-the-Scenes Glimpses

Behind-the-scenes glimpses provide a personal touch that can set your brand apart. Sharing the process of stocking your machines, selecting new products, or even the day-to-day operations of your business can make your brand feel more relatable and trustworthy. These posts can include short videos or photos that show your team in action, highlighting the effort and care that goes into maintaining high standards. By humanizing your brand, you foster a deeper connection with your audience, encouraging loyalty and engagement.

Engaging With Your Audience

Engaging with your audience is crucial for a successful content strategy. Responding to comments and messages promptly shows that you value your followers and are attentive to their needs. Asking questions and encouraging feedback on your posts can also boost engagement. For example, you could ask your followers to vote on new products they'd like to see in your vending machines or to share their favorite snack moments. This interaction not only increases visibility but also provides valuable insights into customer preferences.

Consistency and Planning

To keep your content strategy effective and dynamic, consistency is key. Develop a content calendar to plan and schedule your posts in advance. This helps maintain a regular posting schedule, ensuring your audience always has fresh content to engage with. Use analytics tools provided by social media platforms to track the performance of your posts and adjust your strategy based on what works best. Monitoring metrics like likes, comments, shares, and reach can help you understand what resonates with your audience and refine your approach accordingly.

Promotions and Collaborations

Promotions and collaborations can further enhance your content strategy. Running contests or offering discounts exclusively to your social media followers can drive engagement and attract new customers. Collaborating with local influencers or businesses can also expand your reach and introduce your brand to new audiences. For instance, you could partner with a fitness influencer to promote healthy snack options available in your vending machines, or collaborate with a local business to create joint promotions that benefit both parties.

Building Community Through Engagement

Building a vibrant and engaged community around your vending machine business is essential for long-term success. By encouraging customer interaction through contests, polls, and consistently responding to comments and messages, you can foster a loyal customer base that feels valued and connected to your brand. Here's how to effectively build a community through engagement.

Contests and Giveaways

Running contests and giveaways is a fantastic way to boost engagement and attract new followers. Contests can be as simple or as elaborate as you like, but the key is to make them fun and relevant to your brand. For example, you could ask your followers to share a photo of their favorite snack from your vending machine, tag your business, and use a specific hashtag to enter. Offering an attractive prize, such as a free snack bundle or a gift card, can motivate more people to participate.

Giveaways can also be used to celebrate milestones, such as reaching a certain number of followers or launching a new vending machine location. Announce the giveaway on your social media platforms, and encourage your followers to participate by liking, sharing, and commenting on the post. This not only increases engagement but also expands your reach as more people become aware of your brand through their network.

Interactive Polls

Interactive polls are another effective way to engage with your audience and gather valuable feedback. Use polls to ask your followers about their preferences, such as which new snack they'd like to see in your vending machines or what their favorite healthy snack option is. Instagram Stories, Facebook polls, and Twitter polls are excellent tools for this purpose.

Polls serve a dual purpose, they engage your audience by making them feel involved in decision-making, and they provide you with insights into customer preferences. This information can guide your product selection and marketing strategies, ensuring that you meet your customers' needs and expectations.

Responding to Comments and Messages

Engagement doesn't end with posting content; it extends to how you interact with your followers. Responding to comments and messages promptly and thoughtfully shows that you value your customers and are attentive to their feedback. Whether it's a question about product availability, a compliment, or a complaint, addressing each interaction with care builds trust and loyalty.

Make it a habit to monitor your social media accounts regularly and engage with your followers. Thank customers for their positive feedback, address any concerns or issues they raise, and participate in conversations. This level of engagement not only strengthens your relationship with existing customers but also demonstrates to potential customers that you are responsive and customer-focused.

Creating Engaging Content

Beyond contests and polls, the content you share should encourage interaction. Share stories and posts that invite your followers to comment and share their experiences. For instance, you could post a photo of a new product and ask, "Who's excited to try this new snack? Let us know in the comments!" or share a behind-the-scenes video with the caption, "Here's how we keep our vending machines stocked with your favorite snacks. What's your go-to snack from our machines?"

User-generated content is another powerful way to build community. Encourage your customers to share photos and stories about their experiences with your vending machines, and feature this content on your social media pages. Not only does this provide you with authentic content, but it also makes your customers feel appreciated and recognized.

Leveraging Hashtags

Using relevant hashtags can help increase the visibility of your posts and attract a broader audience. Create a unique hashtag for your brand and encourage your followers to use it when they post about your vending machines. This can create a sense of community among your customers as they see and interact with each other's posts. Additionally, using popular industry-related hashtags can help new customers discover your business.

Building Relationships

Building a community is about forming relationships, not just increasing numbers. Focus on creating meaningful interactions and showing genuine interest in your customers. Highlighting customer stories and testimonials can also build a sense of community. For example, share a post about a loyal customer who enjoys a particular snack from your vending machines, or feature a local business that hosts one of your machines. These stories add a personal touch and create a deeper connection with your audience.

Analytics and Adaptation

Regularly review your engagement metrics to understand what content resonates most with your audience. Tools like Facebook Insights, Instagram Analytics, and Twitter Analytics provide valuable data on how your posts perform, including likes, shares, comments, and overall reach. Use this information to refine your content strategy and focus on what drives the most engagement.

If you notice that certain types of posts, such as contests or polls, generate more interaction, incorporate more of these into your content calendar. Similarly, if responses to comments and messages are well-received, ensure that you continue to prioritize this aspect of your engagement strategy.

Expanding Your Marketing Reach

Paid Advertising Strategies

Expanding your marketing reach through paid advertising on social media can significantly enhance the visibility and profitability of your vending machine business. By targeting specific demographics near your vending machine locations, you can ensure that your ads reach the right audience, driving foot traffic and increasing sales. Here's how to effectively utilize paid social media advertising campaigns to achieve these goals.

Understanding Paid Social Media Advertising

Paid social media advertising involves creating and promoting ads on platforms like Facebook, Instagram, Twitter, and LinkedIn. These platforms offer sophisticated targeting options that allow you to reach specific demographics based on location, age, interests, behaviors, and more. This precision ensures that your marketing efforts are directed towards individuals who are most likely to engage with your vending machines.

Social media platforms have billions of active users, making them an ideal place to promote your business. With the advanced algorithms and data analytics these platforms use, you can target ads to users who have shown interest in similar products or services, ensuring your marketing dollars are spent efficiently.

Setting Clear Objectives

Before launching any paid advertising campaign, it's essential to define your objectives. Common goals for vending machine businesses might include increasing brand awareness, driving traffic to specific locations, or promoting new products. Clear objectives help you create focused and effective ad campaigns.

- *Increasing Brand Awareness:* Aim to make your brand recognizable to a broader audience. This can be particularly useful when entering new markets or introducing new products.
- *Driving Traffic to Specific Locations:* If you have vending machines in particular high-traffic areas, target your ads to increase foot traffic to these locations.
- *Promoting New Products:* When introducing new items in your vending machines, use ads to highlight these offerings and attract customers.
- *Engaging Existing Customers:* Strengthen relationships with current customers by offering loyalty rewards or highlighting new features and products.

Targeting Specific Demographics

The strength of paid social media advertising lies in its ability to target specific demographics. Start by identifying the key demographics for your vending machine locations. For example, if your machines are located in office buildings, your target audience might include working professionals aged 25-50. If your machines are in gyms, you might target fitness enthusiasts aged 18-40.

Use the targeting options available on social media platforms to narrow down your audience. You can target users based on:

- *Location:* Focus on users within a specific radius of your vending machine locations. This ensures that your ads are seen by people who are geographically close and more likely to visit.
- *Age and Gender:* Tailor your ads to the age and gender demographics that match your typical customers.
- *Interests and Behaviors*: Target users based on their interests, such as healthy eating, fitness, or convenience, which align with the products you offer in your vending machines.

Advanced targeting options also allow you to exclude certain demographics that are unlikely to engage with your products, ensuring your ads are shown to the most relevant audiences.

Creating Compelling Ad Content

The success of your paid advertising campaigns largely depends on the quality of your ad content. Your ads should be visually appealing, engaging, and clearly convey the benefits of your vending machines. High-quality images and videos showcasing your products and their convenient locations can attract attention and drive engagement.

- *High-Quality Visuals:* Use professional photos and videos to showcase your products. Ensure the lighting and composition highlight the attractiveness and quality of the items in your vending machines.
- *Engaging Ad Copy:* Craft compelling ad copy that highlights unique selling points, such as the variety of snacks available, the convenience of the locations, or any special promotions. Use clear calls-to-action (CTAs) to encourage users to visit your vending machines or learn more about your products.
- *Storytelling:* Tell a story about your brand or a specific product. This could be a short narrative about how your vending machine products can improve daily life, enhance convenience, or promote health and wellness.

Utilizing Different Ad Formats

Social media platforms offer various ad formats, each with its own advantages. Experiment with different formats to see which works best for your audience and objectives.

- *Image Ads:* Simple yet effective, image ads can highlight specific products or promotions. Use high-quality images with minimal text for maximum impact.
- *Video Ads:* Videos can showcase a range of products, demonstrate the convenience of your vending machines, or tell a story about your brand. Video content often has higher engagement rates than static images.
- *Carousel Ads:* These allow you to display multiple images or videos in a single ad, ideal for showcasing a variety of products or different vending machine locations. Each image or video can have its own link, providing multiple engagement points.
- *Story Ads:* Instagram and Facebook Stories are highly engaging and can be used for time-sensitive promotions

or behind-the-scenes glimpses. Stories are a great way to create urgency with limited-time offers.

Budgeting and Bidding Strategies

Determining your budget and bidding strategy is crucial for maximizing the effectiveness of your paid advertising campaigns. Most social media platforms allow you to set daily or lifetime budgets, ensuring you don't overspend. Start with a modest budget and gradually increase it as you identify what works best.

- *Budget Allocation:* Allocate your budget based on the performance of different ad types and targeting strategies. Monitor which ads generate the highest return on investment (ROI) and adjust your spending accordingly.
- *Bidding Strategies:* Choose a bidding strategy that aligns with your campaign objectives. For example, if your goal is to increase brand awareness, you might opt for cost-per-impression (CPM) bidding. If you aim to drive traffic to your vending machine locations, cost-per-click (CPC) bidding might be more appropriate.

Test different bidding strategies to see which yields the best results. Platforms like Facebook and Instagram offer automated bidding options that can optimize your bids based on your specified goals.

Monitoring and Analyzing Campaign Performance

Regularly monitoring and analyzing the performance of your ad campaigns is essential for optimizing your strategy. Use the analytics tools provided by social media platforms to track key metrics such as impressions, clicks, engagement rates, and conversions.

- *Performance Metrics:* Pay attention to which ads are performing well and which aren't. Metrics such as click-through rates (CTR), conversion rates, and cost per acquisition (CPA) are critical indicators of success.
- *A/B Testing:* Conduct A/B testing with different ad elements (images, copy, CTA) to determine what resonates best with your audience. Use the insights gained to refine your ads.
- *Adjustments:* Analyzing this data helps you understand what resonates with your audience and make informed adjustments to improve your campaigns. For example, if video ads are generating more engagement than image ads, you might allocate more budget towards video content.

Retargeting and Lookalike Audiences

Retargeting allows you to re-engage users who have previously interacted with your ads or visited your website but didn't convert. By reminding these potential customers about your vending machines, you can encourage them to take action. Set up retargeting campaigns to show ads to users who have shown interest but haven't yet made a purchase.

- *Retargeting Strategies:* Use pixel tracking to identify visitors to your website or landing pages and serve them relevant ads. Retargeting can significantly increase conversion rates by keeping your brand top-of-mind for interested users.
- *Lookalike Audiences:* These are users who share similar characteristics with your existing customers. By targeting lookalike audiences, you can expand your reach to new potential customers who are likely to be interested in your vending machines.

Seasonal and Promotional Campaigns

Take advantage of seasonal trends and special occasions to boost your advertising efforts. For instance, promote healthy snacks at the start of the year when many people are focused on health and fitness. Run special promotions during holidays or back-to-school seasons to attract more customers.

- *Seasonal Trends:* Align your advertising campaigns with seasonal trends and events. For example, promote cold beverages and ice cream during the summer, or highlight hot drinks and comfort snacks during the winter.
- *Special Occasions:* Utilize holidays and special occasions to create themed promotions. Valentine's Day, Halloween, and Christmas are excellent opportunities for special offers and themed products.
- *Limited-Time Offers:* Create urgency with limited-time promotions and discounts. Highlight these offers in your ads to encourage immediate action from potential customers.

The Power of Influencer Marketing

Influencer marketing has become a powerful tool for businesses looking to expand their reach and engage with their target audience more effectively. For vending machine businesses, leveraging the influence of local social media personalities can significantly enhance brand visibility and drive customer engagement. Here's a comprehensive guide to utilizing influencer marketing to boost your vending machine business.

Identifying the Right Influencers

The first step in leveraging influencer marketing is identifying the right influencers to partner with. Look for local social media personalities who have a strong following in your target market. These could be fitness enthusiasts, food bloggers, or lifestyle influencers who align with your brand values and appeal to your desired customer base. The key is to find influencers whose followers are likely to be interested in the products offered by your vending machines.

Research and Selection:

- *Local Relevance*: Focus on influencers who have a strong local presence. Their followers are more likely to be within the vicinity of your vending machine locations, making it easier to drive foot traffic.
- *Engagement Rate:* Look for influencers with high engagement rates rather than just a large number of followers. Influencers with active and engaged audiences are more likely to generate meaningful interactions with your brand.
- *Content Alignment:* Ensure the influencer's content style and themes align with your brand. For example, if you offer healthy snacks, partnering with fitness influencers or nutritionists makes sense.
- *Follower Demographics:* Analyze the demographics of the influencer's followers. Ensure they match your target customer profile in terms of age, gender, interests, and location.

Building Authentic Relationships

Once you've identified potential influencers, focus on building authentic relationships with them. Genuine relationships lead to more authentic endorsements, which resonate better with audiences.

Engagement and Interaction:

- *Social Media Interaction*: Engage with their content by liking, commenting, and sharing their posts. This shows that you are genuinely interested in their work and helps build rapport.
- *Personalized Outreach*: When reaching out for a collaboration, personalize your message. Mention specific posts or campaigns they've done that you admire. This demonstrates that you've done your homework and value their influence.

Offer Value in Collaborations:

- *Mutual Benefits:* Clearly outline the benefits for the influencer. This could include free products, exclusive discounts for their followers, or monetary compensation.
- *Creative Freedom:* Allow influencers creative freedom in how they present your products. Authenticity is key, and influencers know how to best engage their audience.
- *Exclusive Access:* Offer influencers early access to new products or special events. This can make them feel valued and more invested in promoting your brand.

Crafting Compelling Campaigns

Work with influencers to create compelling campaigns that highlight your vending machines and products. The goal is to create content that is both engaging and informative, encouraging their followers to take action.

Content Creation:

- *Product Reviews and Demos:* Have influencers review your vending machine products, showcasing the variety and quality. They can demonstrate how easy and convenient it is to use your machines.

- *Behind-the-Scenes Content:* Share behind-the-scenes content of the vending machine operations, such as restocking or maintenance. This can provide an interesting look at the business side of things and build transparency.
- *Challenges and Contests:* Organize challenges or contests where influencers encourage their followers to participate. For example, a "Try a New Snack" challenge can drive more people to visit your vending machines.

Storytelling:

- *Narrative Content:* Encourage influencers to share personal stories about how your vending machines fit into their daily routines. Authentic storytelling can create a deeper connection with their audience.
- *User-Generated Content:* Ask followers to share their experiences with your vending machines using a specific hashtag. This not only creates a sense of community but also provides you with additional content to share.

Leveraging Multiple Platforms

Influencers can help you reach a broader audience by promoting your brand across multiple social media platforms. Each platform has its strengths and can be used to maximize engagement.

Platform-Specific Strategies:

- *Instagram:* Ideal for visually appealing content. Utilize Instagram Stories, Reels, and IGTV for various content formats. Instagram's shopping features can also drive direct sales.

- *TikTok:* Perfect for short, engaging videos. TikTok's algorithm can help your content go viral, reaching a wider audience quickly.
- *Facebook:* Great for more detailed posts and updates. Facebook Groups and Events can also be leveraged for community engagement.
- *Twitter:* Use for real-time updates and customer interactions. Twitter's concise format is excellent for quick announcements and promotions.
- *YouTube:* For long-form content and detailed reviews. Collaborate with influencers to create in-depth product reviews and tutorials.

Tracking and Measuring Success

To ensure your influencer marketing efforts are effective, track and measure the success of your campaigns. Use specific metrics to evaluate the impact of the influencer partnerships.

Key Metrics:

- *Engagement Rates:* Track likes, comments, shares, and saves. High engagement indicates that the content resonates with the audience.
- *Follower Growth:* Monitor changes in your social media following to see if influencer collaborations are driving new followers.
- *Website Traffic:* Use tools like Google Analytics to track how much traffic is coming from influencer posts.
- *Sales Conversions:* Track sales directly linked to influencer campaigns. Discount codes or affiliate links can help measure this.
- *Brand Sentiment:* Analyze comments and mentions to gauge how the campaign is affecting public perception of your brand.

Data Analysis:

- *Campaign Reports:* Create detailed reports for each campaign, highlighting what worked and what didn't. This helps refine future strategies.
- *A/B Testing:* Test different types of content and strategies to see what yields the best results. Adjust your approach based on these insights.

Creating Long-Term Partnerships

While one-off collaborations can provide a temporary boost, creating long-term partnerships with influencers can have a more sustained impact. Long-term partnerships allow influencers to become genuine advocates for your brand.

Benefits of Long-Term Partnerships:

- *Consistent Promotion*: Regular promotion by influencers keeps your brand top-of-mind for their followers.
- *Trust and Credibility:* Long-term collaborations build trust. Followers are more likely to trust recommendations from influencers who consistently endorse a brand.
- *Deeper Integration*: Influencers can integrate your products into their content more naturally over time, making endorsements feel more authentic.

Maintaining Relationships:

- *Regular Communication*: Keep in touch with influencers regularly, even outside of campaign periods. This helps maintain a strong relationship.

- *Exclusive Opportunities:* Offer long-term partners exclusive opportunities, such as first access to new products or involvement in brand decisions.
- *Mutual Feedback:* Encourage open communication and feedback. This ensures that both parties are satisfied and can improve future collaborations.

Engaging Local Communities

Local influencers can also help you engage with specific communities and demographics. By partnering with influencers who are active in local events, fitness clubs, or community groups, you can increase your brand's visibility and relevance within those circles.

Community Engagement Strategies

- *Local Events:* Collaborate with influencers to host or participate in local events. This can increase brand exposure and foster community relations.
- *Community Groups:* Partner with influencers who are leaders in local community groups. They can introduce your brand to a highly engaged audience.
- *Localized Content:* Create content that highlights the local community and how your vending machines serve it. This can make your brand feel more connected to the audience.

Localized Campaigns

- *Seasonal Promotions:* Use local influencers to promote seasonal products or special promotions. For example, a fitness influencer could promote healthy snacks during a local marathon.

- *Customer Spotlights:* Feature local customers in your influencer campaigns. This can create a sense of community and show appreciation for local support.
- *Local Partnerships:* Collaborate with local businesses and influencers for joint promotions. This can help both parties reach new audiences.

Leveraging Traditional Marketing

While digital marketing and social media have become dominant forces in today's marketing landscape, traditional marketing methods still hold significant value, especially for local businesses like vending machine operations. Leveraging traditional marketing strategies such as flyers, posters, and partnerships with local businesses can effectively complement your digital efforts, increasing your brand's visibility and reach.

While digital marketing and social media have become dominant forces in today's marketing landscape, traditional marketing methods still hold significant value, especially for local businesses like vending machine operations. Leveraging traditional marketing strategies such as flyers, posters, and partnerships with local businesses can effectively complement your digital efforts, increasing your brand's visibility and reach. Here's how to maximize these traditional marketing tactics to benefit your vending machine business.

Flyers and Posters

Flyers and posters are cost-effective tools for promoting your vending machines and can be strategically placed to reach your target audience. High-traffic areas such as community centers, schools, gyms, and office buildings are ideal locations for distributing flyers and displaying posters. These marketing materials should be visually appealing and contain key information about your vending machines, including the types of products available, the convenience they offer, and their specific locations.

Design Considerations:

- *Eye-Catching Visuals:* Use high-quality images of your vending machines and the products they offer. Vibrant colors and professional photography can make your flyers and posters stand out.
- *Clear Messaging:* Ensure your message is clear and concise. Highlight the convenience of your vending machines and the variety of products available. Use headlines that grab attention, such as "Fresh Snacks and Drinks at Your Fingertips!"
- *Call-to-Action (CTA):* Include a clear CTA, such as "Visit our vending machine at [location] for your favorite snacks and beverages!" This directs potential customers to take immediate action.
- *QR Codes:* Incorporating QR codes can bridge the gap between traditional and digital marketing by directing potential customers to your website or social media profiles for more information. Make sure the QR code leads to a landing page optimized for mobile devices.

Strategic Placement:

- *Community Centers:* Place flyers and posters in community centers where local events and gatherings occur. This ensures exposure to a wide audience.
- *Schools and Universities***:** Target schools and universities where students and staff look for convenient snack options.
- *Gyms and Fitness Centers:* Highlight healthy snacks available in your vending machines to appeal to health-conscious individuals.

- *Office Buildings*: Provide information about convenient snack and beverage options for busy professionals.

Partnerships With Local Businesses

Forming partnerships with local businesses can be mutually beneficial and enhance your marketing reach. Identify businesses that complement your vending machine products, such as gyms, schools, office complexes, and retail stores. Approach these businesses with a proposal for cross-promotion that highlights the benefits for both parties.

Identifying Potential Partners:

- *Complementary Businesses:* Look for businesses whose clientele matches your target audience. Gyms, schools, and office buildings are ideal candidates.
- *Local Networks:* Utilize local business networks and chambers of commerce to find potential partners. Attend local business events to meet and engage with business owners.

Proposing the Partnership:

- *Win-Win Proposition:* Present a proposal that clearly outlines the mutual benefits. For example, placing your vending machines in the lobby or common areas of an office building provides convenient snack options for employees while generating additional revenue for both parties.
- *Revenue Sharing:* Offer the business a share of the revenue generated by the vending machine. This financial incentive can make the partnership more attractive.

- *Free Products:* Consider providing free products or discounts to the business as part of the agreement. This can foster goodwill and encourage a stronger partnership.

Executing the Partnership:

- *Co-Branded Marketing Materials:* Create flyers, posters, and digital content that feature both your brand and the partnering business. For instance, if you partner with a gym, design posters that highlight how your vending machines offer healthy snacks and drinks ideal for post-workout recovery.
- *In-Store Promotions*: Run joint promotions with your partners. For example, offer a discount on vending machine products to customers who show a receipt from the partnering business.
- *Event Sponsorship:* Sponsor events hosted by your partners. Provide snacks and beverages from your vending machines, and use the opportunity to distribute marketing materials.

Community Involvement

Engaging with the local community through events and sponsorships is another effective traditional marketing strategy. Participate in community events such as fairs, festivals, and sports events by setting up a booth or sponsoring a local team. Distribute flyers and promotional items, and offer free samples from your vending machines to attract attention and generate interest.

Event Participation

- *Local Fairs and Festivals:* Set up a booth at local fairs and festivals to showcase your vending machines. Provide free samples and engage with attendees to explain the benefits of your products.
- *Sports Events:* Sponsor local sports teams and events. Display your branding on team uniforms and event banners. Offering free samples of your snacks and drinks at these events can create a positive association with your brand.

Sponsorships:

- *Youth Sports Teams:* Sponsor a youth sports team and have your logo on their uniforms. This not only increases brand visibility but also shows your support for the community.
- *Community Events:* Sponsor community events such as charity runs, school events, or local concerts. Provide refreshments and distribute promotional materials to engage with attendees.

Benefits of Community Involvement:

- *Brand Loyalty:* Being actively involved in the community fosters a positive image and builds brand loyalty. Residents are more likely to support businesses that contribute to their community.
- *Increased Visibility:* Sponsoring events and participating in community activities increases your brand's visibility and can lead to increased foot traffic to your vending machines.

Direct Mail Campaigns

Direct mail campaigns are another traditional marketing method that can effectively reach potential customers. Design and send out postcards or brochures that introduce your vending machines, highlight their benefits, and include a special offer or discount. Target your mailing to specific neighborhoods or businesses near your vending machine locations to maximize relevance and impact.

Designing Direct Mail Pieces:

- *Appealing Visuals:* Use high-quality images and professional design to make your direct mail pieces stand out. Include pictures of your vending machines and the products they offer.
- *Clear Messaging:* Clearly communicate the benefits of your vending machines. Highlight the convenience, variety of products, and any special promotions.
- *Special Offers:* Include a special offer or discount to incentivize recipients to visit your vending machines. For example, "Enjoy 10% off your next purchase with this postcard."

Targeting the Right Audience:

- *Local Businesses:* Send direct mail pieces to local businesses near your vending machine locations. This can attract employees looking for convenient snack options.
- *Residential Areas:* Target specific neighborhoods that are within a convenient distance to your vending machines. This can increase foot traffic from local residents.

Combining Direct Mail With Digital Elements:

- *QR Codes*: Include QR codes that direct recipients to your website or social media profiles for more information. This can bridge the gap between traditional and digital marketing.
- *Online Follow-Up:* Encourage recipients to follow you on social media for additional promotions and updates. This helps build an ongoing relationship with potential customers.

Tracking and Measuring Success

To ensure the effectiveness of your traditional marketing efforts, track and measure the success of your campaigns. Use unique discount codes or trackable QR codes on your flyers, posters, and direct mail pieces to monitor how many customers are engaging with your promotions. Collect feedback from your partners and customers to understand what works best and where improvements can be made.

Tracking Methods:

- *Unique Codes:* Use unique discount codes for each campaign to track redemption rates. This helps you measure the direct impact of your marketing efforts.
- *QR Codes*: Track the number of scans on your QR codes to see how many recipients are engaging with your digital content.
- *Surveys:* Conduct surveys to gather feedback from customers and partners. Ask about their awareness of your promotions and their overall experience with your vending machines.

Analyzing Results

- *Campaign Reports:* Create detailed reports to analyze the performance of each traditional marketing campaign. Look at metrics such as engagement rates, sales increases, and customer feedback.
- *ROI Analysis:* Calculate the return on investment (ROI) for each campaign to determine which strategies are most cost-effective. Focus on the tactics that yield the highest returns.
- *Continuous Improvement:* Use the insights gained from your analysis to refine your traditional marketing strategies. Continuously improve your approach based on what works best.

Chapter 7
Scaling the Equation: Replicating Success

Once you've established a profitable and efficient vending machine operation, the next logical step is to scale your business. Welcome to "Scaling the Equation: Replicating Success," where we explore how to take your vending machine business to new heights by expanding your network, enhancing operational efficiency, and maintaining consistent quality across all locations.

Imagine the impact of doubling or even tripling the number of vending machines under your management. Each new machine represents not just an increase in revenue, but also an opportunity to reach more customers, diversify your product offerings, and build a stronger brand presence. However, scaling up requires more than just purchasing additional machines; it demands a well-thought-out strategy to ensure that each new location replicates the success of your initial operations.

The journey to scale begins with understanding the financial aspects of expansion. You'll need to explore various funding options to support your growth, whether through reinvesting profits, securing loans, or attracting investors. Financial planning is crucial to avoid overextending your resources and to ensure that every new machine contributes positively to your bottom line.

Growing Your Vending Machine Empire

Financing Your Expansion

Expanding your vending machine business from a single location or a small network to a larger empire requires substantial financial resources. Financing your expansion is a critical step that involves exploring various funding options to add more vending machines to your network. By understanding and leveraging these options, you can ensure a smooth and sustainable growth process.

Reinvesting Profits

One of the most straightforward methods to finance your expansion is by reinvesting profits from your existing vending machines. This approach has the advantage of not requiring external funding, which means you retain full control over your business without taking on debt or diluting ownership. To successfully reinvest profits, it's essential to have a clear understanding of your cash flow and profitability. Regularly review your financial statements to determine how much profit can be allocated towards purchasing new machines and covering associated costs such as inventory and maintenance.

Business Loans

Securing a business loan is a common way to obtain the capital needed for expansion. Various financial institutions, including banks and credit unions, offer business loans specifically tailored for small business growth. To increase your chances of approval, prepare a detailed business plan that outlines your expansion strategy, projected revenue, and how the loan will be used. Be ready to provide financial statements, tax returns, and a good credit history. Business loans can provide a significant amount of funding, but it's crucial to consider the interest rates and repayment terms to ensure they align with your financial capabilities.

Equipment Financing

Equipment financing is another viable option for funding your vending machine expansion. This type of loan is specifically designed for purchasing equipment, including vending machines. The machines themselves often serve as collateral, which can make it easier to secure the loan even if you don't have a strong credit history. Equipment financing typically offers favorable terms, such as lower interest rates and longer repayment periods, making it a cost-effective way to expand your inventory of vending machines.

Small Business Grants

Grants are an excellent source of funding because they don't need to be repaid. Various government programs, non-profit organizations, and private entities offer grants to support small business growth. Research available grants that are relevant to your business, such as those aimed at promoting healthy eating, supporting local businesses, or encouraging entrepreneurship. The application process for grants can be competitive and time-consuming, so it's essential to carefully follow the guidelines and provide comprehensive information about your business and expansion plans.

Angel Investors and Venture Capital

If you're looking for substantial funding and are open to sharing ownership of your business, seeking investment from angel investors or venture capitalists might be the right path. Angel investors are individuals who provide capital in exchange for equity, while venture capital firms offer funding from pooled investments. Both options can provide significant financial resources and valuable business expertise. However, it's crucial to be prepared to give up a portion of ownership and control over your business. Present a compelling business plan, demonstrate your business's growth potential, and be transparent about the risks and rewards to attract potential investors.

Crowdfunding

Crowdfunding has emerged as a popular way to raise funds for business expansion. Platforms like Kickstarter, Indiegogo, and GoFundMe allow you to present your business idea to a large audience and solicit small contributions from individuals. Crowdfunding can also serve as a marketing tool, increasing brand awareness and engaging your customer base. To launch a successful crowdfunding campaign, create a compelling story, offer attractive rewards or incentives for contributors, and actively promote your campaign through social media and other channels.

Leasing Vending Machines

Leasing vending machines is an alternative to purchasing them outright, reducing the upfront capital required for expansion. Leasing agreements typically involve monthly payments over a specified period, allowing you to spread the cost of the machines over time. Some leasing agreements also include maintenance and repair services, which can further reduce operational costs. While leasing can be more expensive in the long run compared to buying machines outright, it provides an affordable way to expand your network without significant initial investment.

Personal Savings and Family Loans

Using personal savings or borrowing from family and friends is another way to finance your expansion. This option avoids the complexities and obligations of formal loans or investments.

However, it's important to approach this method with caution. Treat any loans from family and friends as formal agreements with clear terms and repayment plans to avoid misunderstandings and potential strain on personal relationships.

Building a Strong Team

As your vending machine business expands, building a strong team becomes crucial for maintaining operational efficiency and ensuring customer satisfaction. Identifying key roles and hiring reliable employees are essential steps to support your growth. Here's how to structure your team and implement effective hiring strategies to build a robust workforce for your vending machine empire.

Expanding your vending machine business requires delegating tasks and responsibilities to specialized roles. The primary roles you need to fill include route operators, inventory managers, and maintenance technicians.

Route Operators

Route operators are responsible for restocking vending machines, collecting cash, and ensuring that machines are functioning correctly. They play a critical role in maintaining the daily operations of your vending machines. As the face of your company, route operators should possess excellent organizational skills, a strong work ethic, and the ability to handle cash responsibly. Additionally, they should be familiar with the areas where your vending machines are located to optimize route efficiency.

Inventory Managers

Inventory managers oversee the stock levels of products across all your vending machines. They track inventory usage, manage orders, and ensure that popular items are always available. Effective inventory management helps prevent stockouts and reduces waste from overstocking. Inventory managers should have strong analytical skills, attention to detail, and experience with inventory management software to streamline the process.

Maintenance Technicians

Maintenance technicians handle the upkeep and repair of vending machines. They ensure that machines are clean, functional, and free from technical issues. Regular maintenance helps prevent downtime and extends the lifespan of your machines. Technicians should have a good understanding of the technical aspects of vending machines, problem-solving skills, and the ability to perform routine maintenance tasks efficiently.

Building a reliable team starts with a thorough hiring process. Implementing effective hiring strategies can help you find the right candidates for each role.

Define Clear Job Descriptions

Begin by creating detailed job descriptions that outline the responsibilities, qualifications, and skills required for each position. Clear job descriptions help attract suitable candidates and set expectations for their roles. Include information about the work environment, physical demands, and any special requirements, such as a valid driver's license for route operators.

Utilize Multiple Recruiting Channels

Expand your reach by using multiple recruiting channels to find potential candidates. Post job openings on popular job boards, social media platforms, and your company's website. Networking through industry associations and attending job fairs can also help you connect with qualified candidates. Consider working with staffing agencies that specialize in logistics and operations roles to find skilled workers.

Conduct Thorough Interviews

During the interview process, focus on assessing both technical skills and cultural fit. Prepare a mix of behavioral and situational questions to evaluate how candidates handle various scenarios related to their roles. For example, ask route operators how they would manage a machine breakdown during their route or inventory managers how they would address a sudden spike in product demand. Practical assessments, such as a test route or a problem-solving exercise, can provide additional insights into a candidate's capabilities.

Check References and Backgrounds

Perform thorough reference and background checks to verify the reliability and integrity of potential employees. Contact previous employers to confirm job performance and ask about the candidate's work habits, reliability, and interpersonal skills. Background checks can help identify any issues that might affect their suitability for the role, such as a history of financial mismanagement for route operators.

Offer Competitive Compensation and Benefits

Attract and retain top talent by offering competitive compensation and benefits packages. Research industry standards to ensure your salary offerings are competitive. Consider additional benefits such as health insurance, retirement plans, and performance bonuses. Providing opportunities for career advancement and professional development can also enhance employee satisfaction and loyalty.

Provide Comprehensive Training

Invest in comprehensive training programs to ensure your employees are well-equipped to perform their roles effectively. Training should cover technical skills, company procedures, and customer service standards. For example, route operators should be trained on optimal restocking techniques, cash handling, and customer interaction. Ongoing training and support help employees stay updated on best practices and new technologies.

Foster a Positive Work Environment

Create a positive work environment that encourages collaboration, communication, and respect. Recognize and reward hard work and achievements to boost morale. Foster open communication channels where employees feel comfortable sharing feedback and suggestions. A supportive work culture can enhance job satisfaction and reduce turnover rates.

Delegation and Empowerment

As your vending machine business grows, the ability to delegate tasks and empower your team becomes increasingly important. Effective delegation not only ensures that all aspects of your business are managed efficiently but also fosters a collaborative work environment where employees feel valued and motivated. Here's how to delegate tasks effectively and empower your team to achieve success.

Understanding the Importance of Delegation

Delegation is a crucial skill for any business owner. It allows you to distribute responsibilities, focus on strategic planning, and avoid burnout. By assigning tasks to qualified team members, you can ensure that each aspect of your business receives the attention it needs. Delegation also provides opportunities for your employees to develop new skills and take on more significant roles within the company.

Assigning Tasks Effectively

Effective delegation involves assigning tasks to the right people based on their skills, experience, and interests. Start by assessing the strengths and skills of your team members. Assign tasks that match their expertise and provide opportunities for growth. Clearly outline the tasks and expectations for each role. Provide detailed instructions and set measurable goals to ensure that employees understand what is required of them. Ensure that employees have the tools, resources, and training they need to complete their tasks successfully. This includes access to inventory management software, maintenance equipment, and customer service protocols. Establish realistic deadlines for task completion. Consider the complexity of the task and the employee's workload when setting timelines. Regularly check in with employees to monitor their progress and provide constructive feedback. This helps ensure that tasks are on track and allows for adjustments if needed.

Empowering Your Team

Empowerment goes beyond delegation; it involves giving employees the authority, confidence, and resources to make decisions and take ownership of their work. Empowered employees are more likely to be engaged, motivated, and committed to the success of the business. Give employees the freedom to make decisions within their areas of responsibility. Trust them to handle tasks without micromanaging, and support their decisions. Create a work environment that encourages collaboration and open communication. Hold regular team meetings to discuss progress, share ideas, and address challenges collectively. Acknowledge the hard work and achievements of your employees. Recognition can be in the form of verbal praise, written commendations, or tangible rewards such as bonuses or promotions. Invest in the professional growth of your employees by providing training, mentorship, and opportunities for career advancement. This not only enhances their skills but also shows that you value their contributions. Encourage employees to provide feedback on processes, policies, and overall business operations. This input can lead to improvements and innovations that benefit the entire organization.

Building a Strong Team Culture

A strong team culture is essential for fostering collaboration and empowerment. Promote a culture of respect, inclusivity, and continuous improvement. Encourage employees to share their ideas and take initiative. Celebrate successes together and learn from setbacks as a team.

Maintaining Control as You Grow

Developing Standardized Operating Procedures

As your vending machine business expands, maintaining control and ensuring consistency across all locations becomes increasingly challenging. Developing standardized operating procedures (SOPs) is a critical strategy for addressing these challenges. SOPs provide a framework for consistent operations, helping to maintain efficiency, quality, and customer satisfaction as your business grows.

The Importance of SOPs

Standardized operating procedures are essential for ensuring that every aspect of your vending machine business operates smoothly and consistently. SOPs serve as a comprehensive guide for your employees, detailing how tasks should be performed to achieve uniformity across all locations. This consistency is crucial for building a reliable brand reputation, as customers expect the same level of service and product quality regardless of which vending machine they use.

Creating Effective SOPs

To develop effective SOPs, start by identifying the core processes and tasks that need standardization. These typically include machine restocking, inventory management, cash handling, maintenance, and customer service. Break down each process into clear, step-by-step instructions that are easy to follow. Use simple language and include visual aids, such as diagrams or checklists, to enhance understanding.

Restocking Procedures

Standardizing restocking procedures ensures that all vending machines are consistently stocked with the right products, minimizing stockouts and overstocking. Define specific guidelines for how often machines should be restocked, how to rotate products to maintain freshness, and how to handle expired or damaged items. Include instructions for recording inventory levels and reporting discrepancies to inventory managers.

Inventory Management

Effective inventory management is crucial for maintaining product availability and controlling costs. Develop SOPs that outline how to track inventory levels, place orders with suppliers, and manage stock across multiple locations. Implementing a standardized system for inventory tracking, such as using barcode scanners or inventory management software, can streamline this process and reduce errors.

Cash Handling Procedures

Standardized cash handling procedures are vital for ensuring accuracy and security. Provide detailed instructions on how to collect, count, and deposit cash from vending machines. Include protocols for recording cash collections and addressing discrepancies. Emphasize the importance of security measures, such as transporting cash in secure containers and performing cash counts in a controlled environment.

Maintenance and Troubleshooting

Regular maintenance and prompt troubleshooting are essential for keeping vending machines in good working order. Develop SOPs that specify maintenance schedules, such as weekly cleaning, monthly inspections, and annual servicing. Include guidelines for common troubleshooting tasks, such as addressing coin jams, replacing faulty parts, and resetting machines. Ensure that employees know how to report technical issues and request repairs.

Customer Service Standards

Providing excellent customer service is key to retaining customers and building a positive reputation. Develop SOPs that outline how to handle customer inquiries, complaints, and refunds. Train employees to respond promptly and courteously to customer issues, whether they arise in person, via phone, or through social media. Include protocols for escalating unresolved issues to higher management.

Implementing and Enforcing SOPs

Once your SOPs are developed, it's crucial to implement them effectively and ensure compliance across all locations. Start by training your employees on the new procedures, providing hands-on demonstrations and opportunities for practice. Use training materials such as manuals, videos, and interactive sessions to reinforce learning.

Regularly monitor compliance with SOPs through audits and performance evaluations. Conduct periodic checks to ensure that procedures are being followed correctly and consistently. Provide feedback and additional training as needed to address any gaps or issues.

Continuous Improvement

SOPs should be living documents that evolve with your business. Encourage feedback from employees on the practicality and effectiveness of the procedures. Regularly review and update SOPs to reflect changes in operations, technology, and industry best practices. Involving employees in the revision process can enhance buy-in and ensure that the procedures remain relevant and effective.

Implementing Performance Metrics

Understanding KPIs

Key Performance Indicators (KPIs) are measurable values that demonstrate how effectively a company is achieving its business objectives. For a vending machine business, KPIs help track progress, pinpoint inefficiencies, and make informed decisions. By focusing on specific metrics, you can gain insights into operational performance and identify areas that require attention.

Sales Performance

Sales performance is one of the most critical KPIs for a vending machine business. Tracking sales metrics helps you understand which products are popular, which locations are performing well, and overall revenue trends. Key sales metrics include:

Total Sales Volume: The total number of products sold within a specific period.

Revenue: Total income generated from sales.

Sales per Machine: Average sales per vending machine, providing insight into the performance of individual units.

Product Sales Breakdown: Sales data for each product, identifying best-sellers and underperforming items.

By analyzing these metrics, you can make data-driven decisions about product offerings, pricing strategies, and machine placement. For example, if a particular product consistently underperforms, you might replace it with a new item. Similarly, high-performing locations can be prioritized for future machine placements.

Machine Uptime

Machine uptime is another crucial KPI, reflecting the percentage of time your vending machines are operational and available to customers. High uptime indicates efficient maintenance and fewer technical issues, directly impacting customer satisfaction and sales. Key uptime metrics include:

Uptime Percentage: The ratio of operational time to total time, expressed as a percentage.

Downtime Incidents: The number and duration of downtime events, including maintenance, repairs, and refills.

Response Time: The time taken to address and resolve machine issues.

Maintaining high machine uptime involves regular maintenance, prompt repairs, and efficient restocking. Tracking these metrics helps you identify patterns and areas where your maintenance processes can be improved. For instance, if a particular machine experiences frequent downtime, it may indicate a need for more thorough maintenance or an upgrade.

Customer Satisfaction

Customer satisfaction, though less tangible, is a vital KPI for long-term success. Happy customers are more likely to return and recommend your vending machines to others. Metrics to track customer satisfaction include:

Customer Feedback: Collecting and analyzing feedback through surveys, social media, and direct interactions.

Complaint Resolution Rate: The percentage of customer complaints resolved satisfactorily within a specific timeframe.

Repeat Customers: The number of returning customers, indicating loyalty and satisfaction.

Using these metrics, you can address customer concerns promptly and make improvements that enhance their experience. For example, frequent complaints about product availability might signal a need for more efficient inventory management.

Implementing and Monitoring KPIs

To effectively implement KPIs, start by setting clear, measurable goals for each metric. Use vending management software to automate data collection and reporting, ensuring accurate and timely insights. Regularly review KPI reports to assess performance and identify trends.

Create a dashboard that displays real-time KPI data, making it easy for your team to monitor performance at a glance. Hold regular meetings to discuss KPI results, celebrate successes, and brainstorm solutions for any issues.

Continuous Improvement

KPIs are not static; they should evolve with your business. Continuously review and refine your KPIs to ensure they remain relevant and aligned with your business goals. Encourage your team to provide input on potential improvements and new metrics that could offer valuable insights.

Utilizing Technology for Scalability

Utilizing vending management software and route optimization tools can streamline operations, enhance productivity, and ensure consistent service across all locations. Here's how these technologies can help scale your vending machine empire effectively.

Vending Management Software

Vending management software (VMS) is a comprehensive tool that helps automate and manage various aspects of your vending machine business. It provides real-time data on sales, inventory levels, machine performance, and customer interactions, enabling you to make informed decisions and optimize operations.

Inventory Management

One of the most significant benefits of VMS is its ability to streamline inventory management. The software tracks inventory levels in real-time, alerting you when products are running low or nearing expiration. This ensures that your machines are always stocked with popular items, reducing stockouts and overstocking. Automated inventory tracking also helps in identifying sales trends, allowing you to adjust product offerings based on customer preferences.

Sales Analytics

VMS provides detailed sales analytics, offering insights into the performance of individual machines, products, and locations. By analyzing this data, you can identify high-performing machines and popular products, as well as underperforming ones that may need to be replaced or relocated. Sales analytics also help in setting realistic sales targets and measuring progress towards achieving them.

Maintenance and Alerts

Efficient maintenance is crucial for minimizing downtime and ensuring that your vending machines are always operational. VMS includes features that monitor machine performance and send alerts when issues arise, such as power outages, coin jams, or low product levels. This allows you to address problems promptly, reducing downtime and improving customer satisfaction.

Route Optimization Tools

Route optimization tools are essential for managing the logistics of restocking and servicing your vending machines. These tools use advanced algorithms to plan the most efficient routes for your service personnel, minimizing travel time and fuel costs while maximizing productivity.

Efficient Restocking

By optimizing routes, you can ensure that your machines are restocked promptly and efficiently. Route optimization tools consider factors such as traffic conditions, machine location, and product needs to create the most effective restocking schedule. This reduces the time spent on the road and increases the number of machines that can be serviced in a day.

Cost Savings

Optimizing routes not only improves efficiency but also leads to significant cost savings. Reduced travel time and fuel consumption lower operational costs, while efficient scheduling minimizes labor expenses. These savings can be reinvested into your business to support further growth and expansion.

Enhanced Customer Service

Efficient route planning ensures that your machines are always well-stocked and in good working condition, enhancing the customer experience. Customers are more likely to return to machines that consistently offer their favorite products and function reliably. This leads to increased sales and customer loyalty.

Integration and Scalability

Both VMS and route optimization tools are designed to integrate seamlessly with other business systems, such as accounting and customer relationship management (CRM) software. This integration provides a holistic view of your operations and supports data-driven decision-making. As your business grows, these tools can scale with you, accommodating additional machines and locations without compromising efficiency.

Chapter 8
Investing in Innovation: Staying Ahead of the Curve

Innovation is not just an advantage; it's a necessity. For your vending machine business to thrive and remain competitive, continuously investing in innovation is essential

Vending machines are more than just snack dispensers—they are interactive hubs of convenience, utilizing the latest in technology to provide an unparalleled customer experience. From cashless payment systems and remote monitoring to eco-friendly solutions and smart inventory management, innovation transforms your operations, making them more efficient and customer-friendly.

The journey towards innovation begins with a commitment to staying informed about the latest industry trends and technological advancements. This involves not only keeping an eye on what competitors are doing but also seeking inspiration from other industries. Attending trade shows, participating in industry forums, and subscribing to relevant publications can provide valuable insights and spark new ideas.

Embracing Technological Advancements:

Cashless Payment Systems

The Rise of Cashless Payments

The shift towards cashless payments is undeniable. Mobile wallets like Apple Pay, Google Wallet, and Samsung Pay, along with contactless credit and debit cards, have become mainstream. Consumers appreciate the ease of tapping a card or smartphone to complete transactions quickly and securely. This trend is particularly pronounced among younger generations who are more tech-savvy and prefer digital transactions over cash.

Benefits of Cashless Payment Systems

Convenience for Customers: Cashless payment options offer unparalleled convenience. Customers no longer need to carry cash or worry about having the exact change. This ease of use can lead to increased sales, as the barrier to making a purchase is significantly lowered.

Increased Sales: Studies have shown that consumers tend to spend more when using cashless payment methods compared to cash. The frictionless nature of these transactions can lead to higher sales per transaction and an overall increase in revenue for your vending machines.

Enhanced Security: Cashless transactions reduce the risk of theft and vandalism associated with cash handling. Since there is no physical money involved, the chances of robbery are minimized. Additionally, electronic payments provide an added layer of security through encryption and authentication, protecting both the consumer and the business from fraud.

Operational Efficiency: Managing cash can be time-consuming and costly. It involves regular collection, counting, depositing, and reconciling. By transitioning to cashless payments, you can streamline these processes, reduce errors, and save time and resources. This efficiency allows you to focus more on strategic business growth.

Integrating Cashless Payment Systems

Choosing the Right Technology: Start by selecting the appropriate cashless payment systems that suit your business needs. Look for systems that support multiple payment methods, including mobile wallets and contactless cards. Ensure the technology is reliable, user-friendly, and compatible with your existing vending machines.

Installation and Setup: Once you have chosen the technology, the next step is installation and setup. This process typically involves attaching a card reader or NFC (Near Field Communication) device to your vending machines. Most modern vending machines are designed to accommodate these devices easily. Work with a reputable provider to ensure proper installation and integration.

Vendor Partnerships: Partner with payment processing companies that offer comprehensive support and competitive transaction fees. These companies can provide the necessary hardware, software, and maintenance services. They can also assist with regulatory compliance and security measures to protect against data breaches and fraud.

Training and Support: Train your staff on how to operate and maintain the new payment systems. Ensure they understand how to troubleshoot common issues and assist customers who might be unfamiliar with the technology. Provide ongoing support to address any technical problems that may arise.

Marketing the New Payment Options

Customer Education: Educate your customers about the new payment options available at your vending machines. Use clear signage and instructions on the machines to guide users through the payment process. Highlight the benefits of using cashless payments, such as speed, convenience, and security.

Promotions and Incentives: Launch marketing campaigns to promote the cashless payment options. Offer incentives such as discounts or loyalty rewards for customers who use mobile wallets or contactless cards. These promotions can encourage adoption and increase customer satisfaction.

Monitoring and Optimization

Tracking Transactions: Use vending management software to monitor cashless transactions. This software provides valuable data on sales patterns, transaction volumes, and customer preferences. Analyzing this data helps you understand the impact of cashless payments on your business and identify opportunities for further improvement.

Customer Feedback: Solicit feedback from customers regarding their experience with the new payment options. Address any concerns or suggestions they may have to enhance the user experience. Positive customer feedback can be a powerful marketing tool to attract more users.

Continuous Improvement: Stay updated with the latest advancements in payment technology. The field of cashless payments is constantly evolving, with new features and capabilities being introduced regularly. Continuously assess and upgrade your systems to ensure you offer the best possible service to your customers.

Telematics and Remote Monitoring

Understanding Telematics and Remote Monitoring

Telematics refers to the integration of telecommunications and informatics, allowing machines to send, receive, and store data remotely. In the context of vending machines, telematics systems provide real-time data on machine status, sales, and inventory levels. Remote monitoring involves using this data to oversee machine operations and make informed decisions without the need for physical inspections.

Real-Time Performance Monitoring

Telematics systems provide continuous updates on the operational status of your vending machines. You can monitor key performance indicators (KPIs) such as temperature, power status, and sales data. Immediate alerts for issues like power outages, coin jams, or product malfunctions enable you to address problems promptly, minimizing downtime and ensuring machines are always operational.

Optimized Inventory Management

One of the most significant advantages of remote monitoring is the ability to track inventory levels in real-time. Telematics systems provide detailed data on product sales and stock levels, allowing you to predict when and what products need restocking. This prevents stockouts and overstocking, ensuring that popular items are always available to customers while reducing waste and optimizing supply chain management.

Efficient Maintenance Scheduling

Regular maintenance is crucial for the longevity and reliability of vending machines. Remote monitoring systems can track machine usage and wear, helping you schedule maintenance proactively. Predictive maintenance alerts you to potential issues before they become major problems, reducing repair costs and extending the lifespan of your machines.

Data-Driven Decision Making

The data collected through telematics and remote monitoring provides valuable insights into customer behavior and sales trends. Analyzing this data helps you understand which products are popular, which locations are most profitable, and how seasonal changes affect sales. These insights can guide your marketing strategies, product selection, and expansion plans.

Cost Savings and Increased Efficiency

By reducing the need for frequent physical inspections and optimizing routes for restocking and maintenance, telematics and remote monitoring save time and operational costs. Efficient inventory management minimizes the need for emergency restocking trips, while predictive maintenance reduces unexpected repair expenses.

Implementing Telematics and Remote Monitoring

Select a telematics and remote monitoring system that meets your business needs. Look for solutions that offer comprehensive features such as real-time data tracking, automated alerts, and integration with your existing vending management software. Ensure the system is user-friendly and provides detailed analytics and reporting tools.

Work with your telematics provider to install and set up the monitoring devices on your vending machines. These devices typically include sensors and communication modules that transmit data to a central platform. Ensure proper calibration and testing to guarantee accurate data collection.

Provide training for your staff on how to use the telematics and remote monitoring system effectively. Ensure they understand how to interpret the data, respond to alerts, and utilize the system's features to optimize operations. Continuous training and support can help your team stay updated on new functionalities and best practices.

Regularly review the data collected by your telematics system to identify patterns and areas for improvement. Use the insights to refine your inventory management processes, optimize maintenance schedules, and enhance overall operational efficiency. Stay proactive in addressing any issues and continuously seek ways to leverage the technology for better performance.

Exploring Self-Service Kiosks

Incorporating self-service kiosks into your vending machine business can significantly enhance customer convenience and expand your product offerings. These kiosks provide a versatile and user-friendly interface that caters to modern consumer preferences, offering a range of products beyond traditional vending machine items.

Enhancing Customer Convenience

Self-service kiosks offer a seamless and efficient shopping experience. Customers can browse through a wide array of products, make selections, and complete transactions quickly and easily. The intuitive touch-screen interface simplifies the purchasing process, reducing the time customers spend at the machine and enhancing their overall experience. By minimizing wait times and improving accessibility, self-service kiosks can attract more customers and increase sales.

Expanding Product Offerings

Traditional vending machines are often limited by space and can only offer a restricted selection of items. Self-service kiosks, however, can display a vast inventory of products digitally, allowing customers to choose from a broader range of options. This includes snacks, beverages, personal care items, and even electronics. The ability to offer diverse products not only caters to different customer preferences but also opens up new revenue streams for your business.

Customization and Personalization

Self-service kiosks can be customized to meet the specific needs of your business and customers. For instance, you can program the kiosks to offer product recommendations based on previous purchases or popular items. Personalization features, such as loyalty programs and discounts for frequent customers, can also be integrated, encouraging repeat business and building customer loyalty.

Payment Flexibility

Self-service kiosks support multiple payment methods, including cash, credit/debit cards, and mobile payments. This flexibility ensures that customers can use their preferred payment option, further enhancing convenience. The integration of cashless payment systems, such as mobile wallets and contactless cards, aligns with modern consumer trends and reduces the need for cash handling, thereby improving security and efficiency.

Data Collection and Analysis

One of the significant advantages of self-service kiosks is their ability to collect valuable data on customer behavior and sales trends. By analyzing this data, you can gain insights into which products are most popular, peak purchasing times, and customer preferences. This information can guide inventory management, marketing strategies, and product selection, ensuring that your offerings align with customer demand.

Ease of Maintenance and Management

Self-service kiosks are designed for ease of maintenance and management. They come equipped with remote monitoring capabilities, allowing you to track inventory levels, sales, and machine performance in real-time. This helps in scheduling timely restocks and addressing any technical issues promptly, ensuring that the kiosks are always operational and well-stocked.

Marketing and Promotions

Self-service kiosks can serve as an effective marketing tool. You can display advertisements, promotions, and special offers on the kiosk screens, capturing the attention of customers and encouraging impulse purchases. Interactive features, such as product demonstrations and videos, can also be incorporated to enhance the shopping experience and drive sales.

Adapting to Market Trends

The retail landscape is continuously evolving, with consumers increasingly seeking convenience and speed in their shopping experiences. Self-service kiosks are an excellent way to adapt to these market trends and stay competitive. By providing a modern, efficient, and versatile shopping solution, you can meet the changing expectations of customers and differentiate your business from competitors.

The Power of Data Analytics

Harnessing Sales Data for Insights

Harnessing sales data effectively can provide deep insights into your operations, helping you identify best-selling products, optimize inventory, and understand customer behavior.

Identifying Best-Selling Products

Sales data provides a clear picture of which products are performing well and which are not. By analyzing this data, you can pinpoint your top-selling items and ensure they are always well-stocked. This helps in meeting customer demand consistently and avoiding stockouts. Additionally, understanding product popularity allows you to make informed decisions about product placement and promotions.

For example, if certain snacks or beverages consistently outsell others, consider placing them at eye level or in easily accessible slots within your vending machines. Highlight these products in your marketing efforts, and consider running promotions or discounts to boost sales further.

Optimizing Inventory Management

Effective inventory management is crucial for maintaining product availability and minimizing waste. Sales data analytics enables you to track inventory levels in real-time, ensuring that popular items are restocked promptly and less popular items are phased out. This data-driven approach reduces the risk of overstocking and under-stocking, optimizing your supply chain and inventory costs.

With detailed sales data, you can forecast demand more accurately. For instance, by identifying seasonal trends or peak purchasing times, you can adjust your inventory levels accordingly. If certain products see a spike in sales during specific months or events, you can prepare in advance to meet increased demand.

Understanding Customer Behavior

Sales data offers valuable insights into customer preferences and purchasing patterns. By analyzing this data, you can better understand what drives customer choices and tailor your offerings to meet their needs. For example, you might discover that certain healthy snacks are more popular in gym locations, while traditional snacks perform better in office environments.

This understanding allows you to segment your customer base and customize your product offerings based on location and demographic preferences. Additionally, tracking repeat purchases and customer loyalty can help you develop targeted marketing campaigns and loyalty programs that encourage repeat business.

Enhancing Marketing Strategies

Data analytics can significantly enhance your marketing strategies. By identifying which products are most popular and during which times, you can tailor your promotions to maximize impact. For instance, if sales data shows a particular snack sells well in the afternoon, consider running a "midday munchies" promotion to boost sales during that time.

Furthermore, sales data can help you evaluate the effectiveness of your marketing campaigns. By comparing sales data before and after a promotion, you can determine the campaign's impact and refine your strategies for future efforts.

Improving Operational Efficiency

Leveraging sales data can also improve overall operational efficiency. Real-time monitoring of sales and inventory levels enables you to streamline restocking routes and schedules, reducing labor and transportation costs. By focusing on machines that require immediate attention, you can ensure that your vending machines are always well-stocked and operational, enhancing customer satisfaction.

Implementing Data Analytics Tools

To harness the power of sales data, it's essential to implement robust data analytics tools. These tools can automate data collection, analysis, and reporting, providing you with real-time insights and actionable information. Look for solutions that offer customizable dashboards, detailed reports, and integration with your existing vending management systems.

Data-Driven Marketing Strategies

Understanding Customer Preferences

The first step in data-driven marketing is to gather and analyze customer data to understand their preferences and behaviors. This data can be collected through various sources, such as sales transactions, loyalty programs, and social media interactions. By analyzing this information, you can identify trends and patterns that reveal what your customers like, when they buy, and how they interact with your brand.

For example, if data shows that a particular demographic prefers healthy snacks, you can tailor your marketing messages to high-light these products. Similarly, if sales peak at certain times of the day or during specific seasons, you can plan targeted promotions accordingly.

Personalizing Marketing Campaigns

Personalization is key to effective marketing. Customers are more likely to engage with content that feels relevant and tailored to their needs. Using the insights gained from customer data, you can create personalized marketing campaigns that resonate with your audience.

For instance, segment your customer base into different groups based on their purchasing habits, preferences, and demographics. Each segment can receive customized content that speaks directly to their interests. A fitness enthusiast might receive promotions for protein bars and sports drinks, while an office worker might be targeted with ads for quick snacks and coffee.

Email marketing is a powerful tool for personalization. By sending personalized emails that address the recipient by name and offer tailored product recommendations, you can increase open rates and conversion rates. Additionally, personalized email campaigns can include exclusive discounts, birthday offers, and loyalty rewards, making customers feel valued and appreciated.

Targeting Promotions Effectively

Data-driven marketing allows you to target promotions more precisely. Instead of using a one-size-fits-all approach, you can design promotions that cater to specific customer segments or behaviors. For example, if data indicates that a certain product is popular among young adults, you can create a promotion specifically for that age group, using language and imagery that appeal to them.

Geolocation data is another valuable asset for targeting promotions. By knowing where your customers are located, you can deliver location-based offers that drive foot traffic to your vending machines. For example, send push notifications with special offers to customers who are near one of your vending machine locations.

Leveraging Social Media

Social media platforms are rich sources of customer data and provide excellent opportunities for targeted marketing. Use the data from your social media channels to understand what content resonates with your audience and when they are most active. Create targeted ads that align with these insights and use platform-specific tools to reach your desired audience.

For example, Facebook and Instagram offer advanced targeting options based on demographics, interests, and behaviors. You can create ads that appear to users who have shown interest in similar products or who have engaged with your brand before. Retargeting campaigns can also be effective, reminding users of products they viewed but did not purchase.

Monitoring and Adjusting Campaigns

Data-driven marketing is not a set-it-and-forget-it strategy. Continuously monitor the performance of your marketing campaigns using analytics tools. Track key metrics such as click-through rates, conversion rates, and return on investment (ROI). Analyze this data to identify what's working and what isn't, and adjust your strategies accordingly.

A/B testing is a useful method for refining your campaigns. By testing different versions of an ad or email, you can determine which elements perform best and optimize your campaigns for better results.

Staying Informed about Industry Trends:

Attending industry events, networking with other vending machine business owners, and following relevant publications are essential strategies for keeping up-to-date with market dynamics and emerging opportunities. Here's how to effectively stay informed and leverage industry insights to grow your business.

Attending Industry Events

Industry events such as trade shows, conferences, and expos provide valuable opportunities to learn about the latest innovations, products, and trends in the vending machine industry. These events often feature keynote speakers, panel discussions, and workshops led by industry experts who share their insights and experiences.

By attending these events, you can gain firsthand knowledge about new technologies, payment systems, and product offerings that can enhance your vending machine operations. Additionally, you can observe demonstrations of new equipment and software, allowing you to evaluate their potential impact on your business.

Industry events also provide a platform for networking with manufacturers, suppliers, and service providers. Building relationships with these stakeholders can lead to beneficial partnerships and access to exclusive deals or early access to new products.

Networking With Other Business Owners

Networking with other vending machine business owners is another effective way to stay informed about industry trends. By connecting with peers, you can share experiences, discuss challenges, and exchange ideas on best practices and innovative strategies.

Joining industry associations and participating in local or regional meetups can facilitate these connections. These associations often host events, webinars, and discussion forums where members can collaborate and learn from each other. Being part of a community of like-minded professionals can provide support, inspiration, and valuable insights that can help you navigate the complexities of the vending machine business.

Networking can also lead to collaborative opportunities, such as joint ventures or co-marketing efforts. Partnering with other businesses can help you expand your reach, diversify your product offerings, and increase brand visibility.

Following Relevant Publications

Keeping up with relevant publications is essential for staying informed about industry news, market trends, and regulatory changes. Trade magazines, industry blogs, and online news platforms offer in-depth articles, case studies, and expert opinions that can provide valuable insights.

Subscribe to leading industry publications that cover the vending machine sector, such as Vending Times, Automatic Merchandiser, and VendingMarketWatch. These publications often feature success stories, product reviews, and market analysis that can help you stay ahead of the curve.

In addition to traditional publications, follow industry influencers and thought leaders on social media platforms like LinkedIn and Twitter. These individuals often share timely updates, insights, and analysis that can keep you informed about the latest developments and trends.

Utilizing Online Resources

Online resources such as webinars, podcasts, and virtual conferences have become increasingly popular for staying informed about industry trends. These formats offer flexibility, allowing you to access valuable content from anywhere at any time.

Webinars and podcasts hosted by industry experts can provide deep dives into specific topics, such as new payment technologies, customer engagement strategies, and sustainability practices. Virtual conferences and online training programs offer opportunities for learning and professional development without the need for travel

Implementing Learnings

Staying informed is only valuable if you apply the knowledge and insights gained to your business. Regularly review and assess the information you gather from industry events, networking, and publications. Identify actionable steps that can be integrated into your business strategy to improve operations, enhance customer satisfaction, and drive growth.

For example, if you learn about a new cashless payment system that is gaining popularity, consider evaluating its compatibility with your existing machines and the potential benefits it could bring to your customers. Similarly, if a new product trend is emerging, assess its fit with your customer base and experiment with stocking it in your vending machines.

Chapter 9
Risk Management: Mitigating Challenges

From fluctuating market conditions and economic downturns to operational hiccups and security threats, these challenges can impact your business's profitability and sustainability. Welcome to "Risk Management: Mitigating Challenges," where we will explore strategies to identify, assess, and mitigate the various risks that can affect your vending machine operations.

Without proactive risk management, even the most promising vending machine business can encounter unexpected setbacks that derail its growth and success. This chapter will guide you through the essential steps to safeguard your business against common risks, ensuring that you can continue to thrive and expand despite the uncertainties.

Proactive risk assessment is a critical component of risk management. Conducting regular risk assessments helps you identify potential vulnerabilities and develop strategies to address them before they become significant issues. This involves evaluating your business processes, conducting scenario planning, and continuously monitoring your risk environment.

Anticipating Potential Obstacles:

Market Fluctuations and Economic Downturns

Economic downturns and market fluctuations are inevitable challenges that can significantly impact your vending machine business. Developing strategies to adapt your product offerings and pricing during these periods is crucial for maintaining profitability and sustaining your operations.

Understanding Market Fluctuations and Economic Downturns

Market fluctuations refer to the changes in market conditions that affect supply and demand dynamics, consumer behavior, and overall economic stability. Economic downturns are characterized by reduced consumer spending, increased unemployment, and a general slowdown in economic activity. Both scenarios can lead to decreased sales and profitability for vending machine businesses.

Adapting Product Offerings

One of the most effective ways to navigate economic downturns is by adapting your product offerings to meet changing consumer preferences and budget constraints. Offering a diverse range of products can help you cater to a broader audience. Include budget-friendly options alongside premium products to appeal to customers with varying spending capabilities. For example, you can stock a mix of affordable snacks, beverages, and healthier options to attract cost-conscious consumers.

Introducing value packs is another effective strategy. Bundle products together to create value packs that offer more for less. Value packs give customers the perception of getting a better deal, which can boost sales during economic downturns. For instance, you can create combo deals like a snack and a drink at a discounted price.

Focusing on essentials can also help during economic downturns. Consumers prioritize essential items over luxury products. Stock your vending machines with essential and high-demand items that are likely to remain in demand, such as water, basic snacks, and daily consumables.

Adjusting Pricing Strategies

Pricing plays a critical role in how your vending machine business responds to economic fluctuations. Implementing flexible pricing strategies can help you maintain competitiveness and customer loyalty. Dynamic pricing strategies allow you to adjust prices based on demand, competition, and market conditions. This approach helps you remain competitive while maximizing revenue. For example, you can lower prices during off-peak hours to attract more customers and increase prices during high-demand periods.

Offering discounts and promotions can incentivize customers to make purchases, even during tough economic times. Regular promotions, such as "buy one, get one free" or limited-time discounts, can boost sales and attract new customers.

Implementing loyalty programs that reward repeat customers with discounts, free products, or other incentives can encourage customer retention and create a steady revenue stream. For example, a punch card system that offers a free item after a certain number of purchases can motivate customers to keep returning.

Price anchoring techniques can influence customer perceptions of value. Display higher-priced items alongside more affordable options to make the latter seem like better deals. This psychological pricing strategy can drive sales of your mid-range products.

Enhancing Customer Engagement

During economic downturns, maintaining strong customer relationships is essential. Engaging with your customers and understanding their needs can help you tailor your offerings and pricing strategies more effectively. Gathering customer feedback through surveys, social media, and direct interactions can provide insights into their preferences and pain points, helping you make informed decisions.

Communicating the value and benefits of your products clearly through marketing and promotional materials is crucial. Highlight any cost-saving features, such as discounts, value packs, and loyalty programs.

Improving the overall customer experience by ensuring your vending machines are well-stocked, clean, and easily accessible can also enhance customer engagement. Consider implementing contactless payment options and maintaining regular maintenance to keep machines in optimal working condition.

Machine Breakdowns and Stock Shortages

Implementing preventative maintenance routines and backup plans is essential to minimize downtime and ensure the smooth operation of your machines. Here's how to effectively manage and mitigate these challenges.

Preventative Maintenance Routines

Preventative maintenance is the proactive approach to identifying and addressing potential issues before they result in machine breakdowns. Regular maintenance checks can extend the lifespan of your machines, ensure they operate efficiently, and reduce unexpected failures.

Scheduled Inspections: Establish a routine schedule for inspecting your vending machines. This can be weekly, monthly, or quarterly, depending on the usage and location of each machine. Inspections should cover key components such as coin mechanisms, bill validators, refrigeration units, and product dispensers. Regular checks help in early detection of wear and tear or malfunctioning parts that need repair or replacement.

Cleaning and Upkeep: Keeping your vending machines clean is crucial for both operational efficiency and customer appeal. Regular cleaning prevents the buildup of dirt and debris that can cause mechanical issues. Pay special attention to the coin and bill acceptors, product slots, and any moving parts. Clean the exterior of the machines to maintain a professional appearance and enhance customer experience.

Updating Software: Many modern vending machines are equipped with software that controls various functions. Ensure that this software is regularly updated to the latest versions to benefit from improvements and bug fixes. Updated software can also enhance security features and integrate new functionalities.

Training Staff: Ensure that your staff is trained in basic maintenance tasks and troubleshooting techniques. They should be able to handle minor repairs and recognize signs of potential problems that need professional attention. Providing detailed maintenance checklists can help staff carry out these tasks systematically.

Backup Plans for Machine Breakdowns

Despite the best preventative measures, machine breakdowns can still occur. Having backup plans in place ensures that such incidents cause minimal disruption.

Spare Parts Inventory: Keep an inventory of commonly needed spare parts, such as coin mechanisms, bill acceptors, motors, and refrigeration components. Having these parts readily available allows for quick replacements, minimizing downtime. Establish relationships with reliable suppliers to ensure timely replenishment of your spare parts inventory.

Maintenance Contracts: Partner with professional maintenance services that offer rapid response times. Maintenance contracts with service level agreements (SLAs) can ensure that technicians are available to fix issues promptly, reducing the time your machines are out of service. Choose service providers with a good track record and positive reviews.

Remote Monitoring Systems: Invest in remote monitoring technology that allows you to track the status of your vending machines in real-time. These systems can alert you to issues such as jams, empty slots, or power failures, enabling you to address problems before they escalate. Remote monitoring also helps in optimizing restocking schedules and detecting patterns that may indicate recurring issues.

Backup Machines: For high-traffic locations, consider placing an additional machine as a backup. This can ensure continuous service even if one machine breaks down. Alternatively, keep a few portable machines that can be quickly deployed to locations experiencing frequent issues.

Stock Shortages Management

Stock shortages can lead to customer dissatisfaction and lost sales. Efficient inventory management and backup plans are critical to avoid these scenarios.

Real-Time Inventory Tracking: Use inventory management software that provides real-time data on stock levels. This helps you monitor which products are running low and need replenishment. Automatic alerts can inform you when it's time to restock, ensuring that popular items are always available.

Optimized Restocking Schedules: Analyze sales data to determine the optimal restocking frequency for each machine. High-demand locations may require more frequent restocking, while others may need less frequent visits. Efficient route planning based on this data can reduce the risk of stock shortages.

Supplier Relationships: Maintain strong relationships with your suppliers to ensure timely delivery of products. Establishing agreements with multiple suppliers can provide backup options if one supplier faces delays or shortages.

Diversified Product Range: Stock a diversified range of products to cater to varying customer preferences and mitigate the impact of shortages in specific items. Offering alternative options ensures that customers can always find something they want, even if their preferred product is temporarily unavailable.

Theft and Vandalism

These criminal activities not only result in financial losses but can also damage your brand reputation and customer trust. Here's how to safeguard your assets effectively.

Assessing Vulnerability

Before implementing security measures, it's crucial to assess the vulnerability of your vending machines. Consider factors such as location, foot traffic, and historical incidents of theft or vandalism in the area. Machines placed in isolated or poorly lit areas are more susceptible to criminal activities compared to those in high-traffic, secure locations.

Choosing Secure Locations

One of the most effective ways to prevent theft and vandalism is by placing your vending machines in secure, well-monitored locations. Ideal locations include inside office buildings, schools, hospitals, and other facilities with controlled access and security personnel. Machines placed in high-visibility areas deter potential criminals due to the increased risk of being seen and apprehended.

Reinforced Machine Construction

Investing in vending machines with reinforced construction can significantly reduce the risk of theft and vandalism. Look for machines with heavy-duty steel enclosures, shatterproof glass, and tamper-resistant locks. Reinforced designs make it more challenging for vandals to break into the machines and steal products or cash.

High-Security Locks

Upgrading to high-security locks can provide an additional layer of protection for your vending machines. Use locks that are resistant to picking, drilling, and tampering. Consider electronic locks that can be monitored and controlled remotely, providing real-time alerts if unauthorized access is attempted. Changing locks regularly and using unique keys for each machine can further enhance security.

Surveillance Cameras

Installing surveillance cameras around your vending machines acts as a strong deterrent against theft and vandalism. Ensure cameras are positioned to capture clear footage of anyone approaching or interacting with the machines. High-resolution, night-vision cameras are ideal for recording detailed images in various lighting conditions. Signage indicating the presence of surveillance can also discourage criminal activity.

Alarm Systems

Alarm systems can provide immediate alerts if a vending machine is tampered with or moved. These systems can be connected to local law enforcement or security services for quick response in the event of an incident. Motion sensors, vibration detectors, and tilt alarms can be integrated into the machines to trigger alarms when unusual activity is detected.

Cashless Payment Systems

Implementing cashless payment systems reduces the risk of theft by minimizing the amount of cash stored in the machines. Mobile wallets, contactless cards, and other electronic payment methods are not only convenient for customers but also enhance security. With less cash on hand, the machines become less attractive targets for thieves.

Regular Maintenance and Monitoring

Frequent inspections and maintenance of your vending machines can help detect and address security vulnerabilities early. Regularly emptying cash boxes, checking for signs of tampering, and ensuring all security features are functional are critical steps in preventing theft and vandalism. Remote monitoring systems can provide real-time updates on machine status and alert you to any suspicious activities.

Community Engagement

Building relationships with the community and local businesses can contribute to the security of your vending machines. Engaging with customers and nearby businesses fosters a sense of community vigilance, where individuals are more likely to report suspicious activities. Partnering with local security services and participating in neighborhood watch programs can further enhance protection.

Insurance Coverage

Despite all preventative measures, it's essential to have insurance coverage to mitigate financial losses from theft and vandalism. Insurance policies specifically designed for vending machine businesses can cover the cost of repairs, replacements, and lost revenue. Review your policy regularly to ensure it provides adequate coverage for all potential risks.

Educating Employees

Educating your employees about security protocols is crucial for maintaining a secure operation. Train staff to recognize and respond to potential security threats, such as suspicious behavior around vending machines or signs of tampering. Encourage employees to report any incidents immediately and ensure they are familiar with the procedures for contacting security services or law enforcement.

Building Resilience in Your Business

Maintaining Emergency Funds

One of the key components of a resilient business is maintaining emergency funds. These funds act as a financial safety net, allowing you to address unexpected expenses or periods of downtime without jeopardizing your operations. Here's how to effectively maintain emergency funds and why they are essential for your business.

Understanding the Importance of Emergency Funds

Emergency funds are reserves set aside to cover unforeseen costs and disruptions that can impact your business. These might include sudden equipment failures, significant repairs, natural disasters, theft or vandalism, and economic downturns. Having these funds readily available ensures that you can respond quickly to emergencies, maintain cash flow, and avoid taking on debt under unfavorable conditions.

Determining the Right Amount

The amount you need in your emergency fund depends on several factors, including the size of your business, the number of vending machines you operate, and the typical costs associated with running and maintaining those machines. A common recommendation is to set aside at least three to six months' worth of operating expenses. This amount provides a cushion to cover most short-term financial disruptions.

Start by calculating your average monthly expenses, including inventory purchases, machine maintenance, rent for machine locations, employee wages, and other overhead costs. Multiply this amount by the number of months you want to cover. For example, if your monthly operating expenses are $5,000, you should aim to have an emergency fund of $15,000 to $30,000.

Building Your Emergency Fund

Building an emergency fund requires disciplined saving and careful financial planning. Here are some strategies to help you build and maintain a robust financial safety net:

Allocate a Percentage of Profits: Regularly set aside a portion of your profits specifically for your emergency fund. Treat this allocation as a non-negotiable business expense. Automating these transfers to a separate savings account can ensure consistency and discipline.

Reduce Unnecessary Expenses: Review your current expenses and identify areas where you can cut costs. Redirect these savings into your emergency fund. This might include renegotiating supplier contracts, reducing energy consumption, or finding more cost-effective marketing strategies.

Increase Revenue Streams: Explore opportunities to increase your revenue. This could involve expanding your product offerings, entering new locations, or implementing promotions and discounts to boost sales. The additional income can accelerate the growth of your emergency fund.

Use Windfalls Wisely: Direct any unexpected income, such as tax refunds, bonuses, or higher-than-expected sales, into your emergency fund. This approach can significantly bolster your reserves without impacting your regular cash flow.

Managing Your Emergency Fund

Once your emergency fund is established, managing it effectively is essential to ensure it remains available when needed:

Keep Funds Accessible: Store your emergency funds in a liquid account, such as a business savings account, where they can be easily accessed in an emergency. Avoid investing these funds in high-risk or illiquid assets that may not be readily available when needed.

Separate From Operating Funds: Maintain a clear distinction between your emergency funds and regular operating funds. This separation prevents the temptation to use these reserves for non-emergency expenses and ensures they are preserved for their intended purpose.

Regularly Reevaluate Needs: Periodically review and adjust the size of your emergency fund to reflect changes in your business. As your business grows or your expenses change, you may need to increase the amount set aside to ensure adequate coverage.

Replenish After Use: If you need to dip into your emergency fund, prioritize replenishing it as soon as possible. Treat the replenishment process with the same discipline as you did when initially building the fund.

Benefits of a Well-Maintained Emergency Fund

Having a well-maintained emergency fund offers several significant benefits for your vending machine business:

Financial Stability: Emergency funds provide a buffer that allows you to manage unexpected costs without disrupting your regular operations or compromising your financial stability.

Avoiding High-Interest Debt: By relying on your emergency fund instead of high-interest loans or credit cards during a crisis, you can avoid additional financial strain and interest costs.

Peace of Mind: Knowing you have a financial safety net in place reduces stress and allows you to focus on long-term business growth and strategic planning, rather than being preoccupied with short-term financial crises.

Flexibility and Agility: Emergency funds give you the flexibility to respond quickly to opportunities and challenges. Whether it's repairing a broken machine promptly or taking advantage of a sudden market opportunity, having cash on hand allows you to act decisively.

Insurance Coverage

Understanding the Importance of Insurance

Insurance serves as a safety net, covering costs associated with various risks that could impact your vending machines. These risks include physical damage from vandalism or accidents, theft, liability claims, and even natural disasters. Without adequate insurance, you could face significant financial burdens that might jeopardize your business operations.

Types of Insurance Coverage

Property insurance covers physical damage to your vending machines caused by events such as fire, vandalism, or natural disasters. Theft insurance provides coverage for stolen money, products, and parts, helping you recover financially from such incidents. Liability insurance protects you against claims made by third parties for injuries or damages related to your vending machines. Business interruption insurance compensates for lost income if your business operations are disrupted due to insured events like fire or natural disasters. Equipment breakdown insurance covers the costs associated with repairing or replacing vending machines that break down due to mechanical or electrical failures.

Choosing the Right Insurance Provider

When selecting an insurance provider, consider the following factors to ensure you get the best coverage for your vending machine business. Choose a provider with a solid reputation for reliability and prompt claims processing. Ensure that the provider offers comprehensive coverage options tailored to the specific needs of your business. Compare premiums and deductibles from different providers to find a balance between cost and coverage. Excellent customer service is essential for a smooth claims process.

Implementing and Managing Your Insurance

Once you've selected the right insurance coverage, it's important to manage your policies effectively. Periodically review your insurance policies to ensure they still meet your business needs. Keep detailed records of all your vending machines, including purchase receipts, maintenance logs, and an inventory of stocked products. Implement risk management practices to minimize the likelihood of incidents. This includes regular maintenance, secure machine placements, and employee training on handling and reporting issues. Effective risk management can also help lower your insurance premiums.

Building Positive Relationships With Vendors and Repair Technicians

Strong partnerships can enhance your business's efficiency, reduce operational costs, and improve customer satisfaction. Here's how to foster these vital relationships.

Identifying Reliable Vendors and Technicians

The first step in building positive relationships is identifying reliable vendors and repair technicians. Look for vendors who offer high-quality products, competitive pricing, and consistent supply chains. For repair technicians, prioritize those with a solid reputation, proven expertise, and quick response times. Seeking recommendations from other vending machine operators and industry networks can help you find trustworthy partners.

Establishing Clear Communication

Effective communication is the cornerstone of any strong business relationship. Establish clear and open lines of communication with your vendors and technicians. Regularly update them on your needs and expectations, and encourage them to share any concerns or suggestions. Clear communication ensures that both parties are on the same page and can work together seamlessly to address any issues that arise.

Setting Expectations

From the outset, set clear expectations regarding quality, delivery times, pricing, and service standards. Create detailed agreements or contracts that outline these expectations to avoid misunderstandings and ensure accountability. Clearly defined expectations help build trust and ensure that both parties are committed to maintaining high standards.

Consistent Ordering and Scheduling

Consistency in ordering and scheduling demonstrates reliability and helps build strong relationships. Regular, predictable orders with vendors can lead to better pricing and priority service. Similarly, scheduling regular maintenance with your repair technicians ensures that your machines are always in good working condition and helps prevent unexpected breakdowns.

Timely Payments and Professionalism

Timely payments are crucial for maintaining positive relationships with your vendors and technicians. Ensure that you pay invoices promptly and address any billing issues quickly. Professionalism in all interactions—whether negotiating contracts, placing orders, or requesting repairs—fosters respect and a positive working relationship.

Feedback and Continuous Improvement

Providing constructive feedback to your vendors and technicians helps them understand your business needs better and encourages continuous improvement. Similarly, be open to feedback from them. This two-way communication can lead to improved products, services, and processes that benefit both parties.

Building Long-Term Partnerships

Focus on building long-term partnerships rather than transactional relationships. Long-term partners are more likely to go the extra mile to support your business. They may offer better pricing, faster delivery, or priority repair services. Cultivate these relationships by demonstrating loyalty, reliability, and mutual respect.

Training and Knowledge Sharing

Investing in training and knowledge sharing can strengthen your partnerships. Invite vendors and technicians to train your staff on the latest products and maintenance techniques. This collaboration not only improves your team's skills but also shows your partners that you value their expertise and are committed to working closely with them.

Leveraging Technology

Utilize technology to streamline communication and operations with your vendors and technicians. Implement systems that allow for easy order tracking, inventory management, and maintenance scheduling. Technology can facilitate better coordination, reduce errors, and enhance overall efficiency.

Recognizing and Appreciating Partners

Show appreciation for your vendors and technicians by recognizing their efforts and contributions. Simple gestures like thank-you notes, positive reviews, or highlighting their services on your website can go a long way in building goodwill. Acknowledging their hard work fosters a positive and supportive relationship.

Chapter 10
The $500,000 Formula

Setting a clear revenue target is the foundation of your business strategy. Defining the goal of $500,000 per year requires precise planning and an understanding of how to translate this annual figure into achievable monthly and daily targets. This section will help you clarify your financial aspirations and break down the big picture into smaller, actionable steps.

To reach this significant revenue milestone, it's essential to understand the building blocks that will get you there. Calculating the average revenue generated per vending machine per day and determining the number of machines needed to meet your daily revenue target are critical steps. This approach ensures that your growth strategy is grounded in realistic and data-driven projections.

"The $500,000 Formula" is more than just a financial target; it's a comprehensive business strategy designed to propel your vending machine business to new heights. By following the steps outlined in this chapter, you can systematically build a robust and profitable vending machine network, achieving and surpassing your revenue goals.

Setting the Target

Defining Your Goals

Financial aspirations are essential, but what does vending machine success look like for you? Maybe you want to replace your current income entirely, or perhaps generate additional income for a more flexible lifestyle. Do you have specific vending machine goals, like focusing on healthy snacks in a specific region? Whatever your vision is, clearly define it. This clarity will be your roadmap and fuel your journey.

The $500,000 Vending Machine Dream

Don't get overwhelmed by the number – we'll break it down into manageable steps throughout. Think of $500,000 as your ultimate vending machine empire, built through strategic planning, prime locations, and understanding your customers.

Why $500,000? It's a substantial and achievable goal. Remember, you can always adjust it based on your needs and progress. However, a high target from the outset motivates strategic decisions and helps you build a scalable vending machine network.

This sets the stage for your entrepreneurial spirit. By defining your vending machine goals and setting a bold target, you've taken the first crucial step towards building a lucrative business.

Understanding the Breakdown

To achieve an annual revenue goal of $500,000, it's essential to break it down into manageable and actionable monthly and daily targets. This process helps in setting clear expectations and enables precise planning and execution.

Monthly Targets

Start by dividing the annual goal by 12 months.

This means your business needs to generate $41,667 each month to stay on track.

Daily Targets

Next, break down the monthly target into daily targets. Assuming your vending machines operate every day, divide the monthly target by the average number of days in a month, typically 30.

Thus, your daily revenue target is approximately $1,389.

Per Machine Revenue Calculation

To further refine your strategy, determine the average revenue each vending machine should generate daily. If you have 50 vending machines, divide the daily revenue target by the number of machines.

Each vending machine needs to generate about $28 per day to meet the overall goal.

Monitoring and Adjusting

Regularly track your machines' performance to ensure each meets or exceeds the daily target. If certain machines underperform, investigate and address potential issues like location, product mix, or pricing. Conversely, identify and replicate the practices of high-performing machines.

Building Blocks

it's crucial to understand the revenue-generating capability of each vending machine. This begins with calculating the average revenue generated per vending machine per day.

Base Revenue Calculation

Step 1: Gather Data

Start by collecting data from your existing vending machines. This data should include:

Daily sales figures for each machine over a period (preferably several months to account for variability).

Number of transactions per day.

Average transaction value.

Step 2: Calculate Daily Revenue

For accurate calculations, sum up the daily sales figures for each machine and then find the average. For instance, if you have data for 30 days, add the total revenue for those days and divide by 30.

Example:

Machine A: Total revenue over 30 days = $3,000

Average daily revenue = $3,000 / 30 = $100

Repeat this for each machine to get a comprehensive understanding of individual performance.

Step 3: Determine the Overall Average

To find the overall average daily revenue per machine, sum the average daily revenues of all machines and divide by the number of machines.

Example:

If you have 10 machines with average daily revenues of $100, $90, $110, $95, $85, $105, $100, $95, $90, and $105:

Total average daily revenue = $975

Overall average daily revenue = $975 / 10 = $97.50

This figure represents the average daily revenue you can expect per vending machine, serving as a benchmark for further calculations and assessments.

Scalability Assessment:

With the average daily revenue per machine calculated, the next step is to assess scalability – specifically, how many vending machines are needed to achieve your daily revenue target, which is derived from your annual goal.

Step 1: Establish Daily Revenue Target

As established earlier, the daily revenue target to reach $500,000 annually is approximately $1,389.

Step 2: Calculate Required Number of Machines

Divide the daily revenue target by the average daily revenue per machine to determine how many machines are needed.

Example:

Daily revenue target = $1,389

Average daily revenue per machine = $97.50

Required number of machines = $1,389 / $97.50 ≈ 14.24

Since you can't operate a fraction of a machine, round up to the next whole number. Thus, you'll need at least 15 vending machines to meet the daily revenue target.

Step 3: Consideration for Variability

Account for variability and potential underperformance by adding a buffer. If some machines perform below average, having extra machines ensures you still meet your target. Adding a buffer of 10-20% is prudent.

Example:

Buffer: 20% of 15 machines = 3 machines

Total machines needed = 15 + 3 = 18

Step 4: Scalability Plan

Develop a plan to scale up to the required number of machines. This includes:

Evaluating and selecting high-traffic locations.

Securing financing for purchasing additional machines.

Setting a timeline for deploying new machines.

Step 5: Ongoing Monitoring and Adjustment

Regularly monitor the performance of your vending machines. Adjust the number of machines as necessary based on performance data. If some machines consistently outperform others, focus on replicating their success factors in new locations or underperforming machines.

Location Strategy

High-Traffic Locations

The location of your vending machines is one of the most critical factors in determining their success. High-traffic locations are essential for maximizing sales potential, as they ensure a steady stream of potential customers. Here's how to identify and secure prime locations for your vending machines.

Identifying High-Traffic Locations

Begin by researching various locations where people frequently gather. Some ideal spots include:

Office Buildings: Employees often seek quick snacks or beverages, making office buildings an excellent choice.

Schools and Universities: Students and staff provide a constant demand for snacks and drinks.

Hospitals: Visitors and healthcare workers are always in need of refreshments.

Public Transportation Hubs: Train stations, bus terminals, and airports have high foot traffic.

Retail Stores and Malls: Shoppers looking for a quick refreshment can boost your sales.

Gyms and Fitness Centers: Health-conscious individuals often look for healthy snack options.

Securing Prime Locations

Once you've identified potential high-traffic locations, the next step is to secure these spots. Here are some strategies:

Negotiation: Approach property owners or managers with a proposal highlighting the benefits of having a vending machine on their premises, such as convenience for their visitors and potential revenue sharing.

Revenue Sharing Agreements: Offer a percentage of the sales revenue to the location owner as an incentive.

Trial Periods: Propose a trial period to demonstrate the value and low maintenance of your vending machines.

Networking: Leverage existing business relationships and attend local business networking events to find new location opportunities.

Professionalism: Maintain a professional approach in all communications to build trust and secure prime spots.

Location ROI Analysis

Evaluating the ROI of each vending machine location ensures that your investments are yielding profitable returns. Here's how to conduct a thorough location ROI analysis.

Collect Historical Data

If you have existing machines, start by collecting historical sales data from each location. Key metrics include:

Total Sales Revenue: Track monthly and annual sales figures.

Operating Costs: Include costs such as rent, maintenance, restocking, and utilities.

Net Profit: Calculate the net profit by subtracting operating costs from total sales revenue.

Project Future Performance

For new locations, make projections based on similar existing locations or industry benchmarks. Consider factors like:

Foot Traffic Estimates: Use data from similar locations to estimate potential customer volume.

Demographics: Understand the profile of potential customers in the area (e.g., age, income, lifestyle).

Competitor Analysis: Assess the presence and performance of competitors in the area.

Calculate ROI

To calculate ROI, use the formula:

ROI=Net Profit/Total Investment×100

For example, if a vending machine generates $2,000 in net profit annually and the total investment (including purchase, installation, and operating costs) is $10,000, the ROI would be:

$$ROI = 2,000/10,000 \times 100 = 20\%$$

Evaluate and Compare Locations

Compare the ROI of different locations to identify the most profitable ones. Focus on locations with high ROI and consider relocating or optimizing underperforming machines.

Continuous Monitoring and Adjustment

Regularly monitor the performance of each vending machine location. Collect ongoing sales and cost data to reassess ROI periodically. Be prepared to make adjustments, such as changing product offerings or relocating machines, to maximize profitability.

Product Mix Optimization

Product Profitability Analysis

Optimizing the product mix in your vending machines starts with a detailed profitability analysis of each item you offer. To do this, collect data on sales volume and profit margins for all products.

Sales Volume

Track how frequently each product is sold over a specific period. Products with high sales volume are popular and likely drive significant revenue.

Profit Margin

Calculate the profit margin for each product by subtracting the cost of goods sold (COGS) from the sales price, then dividing by the sales price.

Profit Margin=Sales Price−COGS/Sales Price×100

Profitability Assessment

Combine the sales volume and profit margin data to determine overall profitability. Products with high sales volume and high profit margins are ideal. Products with low profitability may need to be replaced or adjusted.

Diversification Strategy

Once you understand the profitability of each product, implement a diversification strategy to cater to a broad range of consumer preferences and maximize overall profitability.

Cater to Diverse Preferences:

Include a variety of products such as snacks, beverages, healthy options, and specialty items to appeal to different tastes and dietary needs. This attracts a wider customer base and increases overall sales.

Balance High and Low-Margin Products

Maintain a balance between high-margin items that drive profit and popular, lower-margin items that attract customers. This mix ensures profitability while meeting customer demand.

Seasonal and Trend-Based Products

Adjust your product offerings based on seasonal trends and emerging consumer preferences. For example, offer cold beverages in summer and hot drinks in winter, or introduce trending snacks that customers are likely to try.

Continuous Monitoring and Adjustment:

Regularly review sales data to identify changing consumer preferences and adjust the product mix accordingly. This dynamic approach ensures your vending machines always offer popular and profitable items.

Marketing and Promotion

Brand Visibility

Increasing brand visibility is essential for attracting customers to your vending machines and building a strong, recognizable brand. Start by ensuring that each vending machine features clear and attractive signage. Use bright, eye-catching colors and bold fonts to make your brand stand out. Place your logo prominently on every machine to reinforce brand recognition.

Branding Elements

Incorporate consistent branding elements such as color schemes, fonts, and imagery across all your machines. This creates a cohesive look that customers can easily identify. Use high-quality graphics and wraps to make your machines visually appealing and professional.

Marketing Collateral

Include marketing collateral such as posters, flyers, and digital screens that display promotional messages and product information. Highlight unique selling points, such as healthy options or locally sourced products, to attract specific customer segments.

Location-Specific Branding

Tailor your branding efforts to suit the location. For example, use themes and messages that resonate with office workers in corporate settings or students in educational institutions.

Promotional Campaigns

Promotional campaigns are powerful tools for driving sales and increasing customer engagement. Implement a variety of strategies to keep customers interested and encourage repeat purchases.

Discounts

Offer discounts on popular items to attract more customers. Use tactics like "buy one, get one free" or percentage discounts on bulk purchases to incentivize larger sales.

Bundle Deals

Create bundle deals that combine complementary products at a discounted rate. For example, offer a snack and a beverage combo at a reduced price. This encourages customers to buy more and increases the average transaction value.

Limited-Time Offers

Introduce limited-time offers to create a sense of urgency. Promotions like "monthly specials" or "seasonal discounts" can boost sales during specific periods. Highlight these offers through signage on your vending machines and digital marketing channels.

Loyalty Programs

Consider implementing a loyalty program where customers earn points or rewards for frequent purchases. This encourages repeat business and builds customer loyalty.

Operational Efficiency

Inventory Management

Effective inventory management is crucial for ensuring that your vending machines are always stocked with popular items while minimizing costs. To achieve this, implement the following practices:

Automated Inventory Tracking

Utilize vending management software that provides real-time data on inventory levels. This technology helps you monitor stock levels, predict demand, and automate restocking schedules.

Just-In-Time Inventory

Adopt a just-in-time (JIT) inventory system to reduce holding costs. By aligning restocking schedules closely with actual sales data, you can minimize the amount of inventory stored in your machines, reducing waste and associated costs.

Stock Prioritization

Focus on stocking high-demand items that sell quickly. Regularly review sales data to identify top-selling products and adjust your inventory accordingly. This ensures that your machines are stocked with items that generate the most revenue.

Supplier Relationships

Build strong relationships with reliable suppliers to ensure timely delivery of products. Negotiate favorable terms and establish consistent delivery schedules to maintain optimal inventory levels.

Route Optimization

Efficient route optimization is essential for reducing operational costs and improving service reliability. Here's how to optimize your vending machine routes:

Route Planning Software:

Use route planning software to design the most efficient paths for servicing your vending machines. This software considers factors such as traffic patterns, machine locations, and service frequency to minimize travel time and fuel costs.

Cluster Servicing:

Group machines located in close proximity to each other into clusters. This approach allows service personnel to restock and maintain multiple machines within a single trip, reducing overall travel time and increasing efficiency.

Dynamic Scheduling:

Implement dynamic scheduling that adjusts service routes based on real-time data. Prioritize machines with low stock levels or high sales volume to ensure timely restocking and maintenance.

Performance Monitoring:

Continuously monitor the performance of your routes and make adjustments as needed. Use data analytics to identify inefficiencies and opportunities for improvement, ensuring that your routes remain optimal over time.

By implementing efficient inventory management practices and optimizing your service routes, you can minimize operational costs, ensure that your vending machines are always well-stocked, and enhance overall service reliability. This focus on operational efficiency will contribute significantly to the profitability and scalability of your vending machine business.

Technology Integration

Cashless Payment Solutions

Mobile Payment Apps

Enable your vending machines to accept mobile payments through popular apps like Apple Pay, Google Wallet, and Samsung Pay. These apps allow customers to make quick, secure payments using their smartphones, reducing the need for cash and enhancing the overall user experience.

Contactless Cards

Equip your machines with contactless card readers that accept payments via credit and debit cards with a simple tap. This technology speeds up the transaction process and caters to the growing number of consumers who prefer contactless payments for their convenience and security.

Benefits

Cashless payment solutions reduce the risk of theft and vandalism, as there is less cash stored in the machines. They also streamline the payment process, making it more convenient for customers and potentially increasing the frequency of purchases.

Data Analytics Utilization

Leveraging data analytics can transform your vending machine business by providing actionable insights into various aspects of your operations.

Consumer Behavior

Analyze transaction data to understand consumer preferences and buying patterns. This information helps you tailor product offerings to meet customer demand more effectively, increasing sales and customer satisfaction.

Product Performance

Track sales data for each product to identify best-sellers and underperforming items. Use these insights to optimize your product mix, ensuring that your machines are stocked with items that maximize profitability.

Operational Efficiency

Monitor machine performance and maintenance needs through data analytics. Predictive analytics can alert you to potential issues before they become critical, reducing downtime and maintenance costs. Additionally, data-driven insights can help you optimize inventory management and restocking schedules, minimizing stockouts and excess inventory.

Implementation

Utilize vending management software that integrates with your machines to collect and analyze data in real-time. Regularly review and act on these insights to improve your business operations continuously.

Continuous Improvement

Performance Monitoring

Continuous improvement begins with regular performance monitoring. Tracking key performance indicators (KPIs) provides insights into your business's health and highlights areas needing enhancement.

Sales Metrics

Regularly analyze sales data from your vending machines. Identify trends in product popularity, peak purchasing times, and overall sales volume. Use this data to adjust inventory and marketing strategies, ensuring high-demand products are always available and promoted effectively.

Profit Margins

Monitor profit margins to ensure your pricing strategy is effective. Compare the cost of goods sold (COGS) with sales prices to identify products with the highest profitability. Adjust your product mix to focus on high-margin items while phasing out less profitable options.

Machine Uptime

Track the operational status of your machines. High machine uptime ensures customer satisfaction and consistent revenue. Regular maintenance and timely repairs are essential to minimize downtime. Use performance data to schedule preventative maintenance and address recurring issues promptly.

By consistently monitoring these KPIs, you can make informed decisions that drive business growth and operational efficiency.

Adaptation and Innovation

Product Offerings

Regularly review and update your product lineup to reflect changing consumer preferences. Introduce new and trending items, such as healthy snacks or eco-friendly products, to attract diverse customer segments. Seasonal and limited-time offerings can also boost interest and sales.

Marketing Strategies

Innovate your marketing approaches to engage customers effectively. Utilize social media, targeted promotions, and loyalty programs to build brand loyalty and drive repeat business. Continuously evaluate the effectiveness of your marketing campaigns and adjust them based on performance data.

Operational Processes

Embrace new technologies and methods to enhance operational efficiency. Implement advanced inventory management systems, cashless payment solutions, and route optimization software. Staying updated with the latest industry trends and technological advancements can streamline your operations and reduce costs.

Agility

Foster a culture of agility within your business. Encourage feedback from employees and customers to identify potential improvements. Be prepared to pivot your strategies quickly in response to market changes or new opportunities.

Financial Management

Cost Control Measures

Bulk Purchasing

Buy products in bulk to take advantage of volume discounts. This approach lowers the cost per unit and increases your profit margins. Establish strong relationships with suppliers to negotiate better terms and prices.

Energy-Efficient Equipment

Invest in energy-efficient vending machines and components. Modern machines with energy-saving features can significantly reduce electricity consumption, leading to lower utility bills.

Look for machines with LED lighting, efficient cooling systems, and programmable energy-saving modes.

Minimizing Overhead Expenses

Identify and reduce unnecessary overhead costs. Streamline operations by optimizing your supply chain, reducing waste, and automating processes where possible. Regularly review your expenses to identify areas where you can cut costs without compromising service quality.

Profit Reinvestment

Reinvesting profits strategically is essential for the growth and long-term success of your vending machine business. Allocating funds to key areas can enhance your operations and expand your market reach.

Expanding the Vending Machine Network

Use a portion of your profits to purchase additional vending machines and secure new high-traffic locations. Expanding your network increases revenue potential and market presence. Prioritize locations with high foot traffic and low competition to maximize returns.

Improving Technology Infrastructure

Invest in advanced technologies to streamline operations and enhance customer experience. Upgrading to cashless payment systems, remote monitoring, and data analytics tools can improve efficiency, reduce downtime, and provide valuable insights into consumer behavior and machine performance.

Marketing Initiatives

Allocate funds to marketing campaigns that boost brand visibility and attract new customers. Effective marketing strategies include social media promotions, loyalty programs, and targeted advertising. Enhanced marketing efforts can drive sales and build a loyal customer base.

Review and Adjust

Performance Evaluation

Regular Reviews

Schedule monthly or quarterly reviews to assess your progress towards the $500,000 target. Analyze key performance indicators (KPIs) such as total sales, profit margins, machine uptime, and customer satisfaction. Compare actual performance against your targets to identify any gaps.

Identify Issues

Look for patterns and trends in your data to pinpoint underperforming machines, products, or locations. Determine the root causes of any issues, whether they are related to inventory management, machine maintenance, or customer preferences.

Adjust Strategies

Based on your performance reviews, make necessary adjustments to your strategies. This could involve changing product offerings, optimizing machine placements, refining marketing campaigns, or enhancing operational processes. Be proactive in addressing issues and implementing changes to keep your business moving towards its revenue goals.

Continuous Learning:

Industry Trends

Keep abreast of the latest industry trends and consumer preferences. Follow industry publications, attend trade shows, and participate in professional networks to gather insights and stay ahead of market changes.

Best Practices

Learn from other successful vending machine operators and businesses. Adopt best practices in areas such as inventory management, customer service, and technology integration to enhance your operations.

Emerging Technologies

Embrace new technologies that can improve efficiency and customer experience. Innovations like advanced payment systems, remote monitoring, and data analytics can provide a competitive edge and drive business growth.

Refinement and Optimization

Regularly update your strategies based on new information and technological advancements. Continuously refine your approach to maximize profitability and operational efficiency.

Chapter 11
Sustaining Success: The Art of Perpetual Growth

Success in the vending machine business doesn't end with reaching your revenue goals; it's about sustaining that success and fostering continuous growth. Achieving significant milestones, like hitting the $500,000 revenue mark, is a testament to your hard work, strategic planning, and adaptability. However, the real challenge lies in maintaining that level of success and leveraging it as a foundation for future growth. Sustaining success in the vending machine business requires a holistic approach that encompasses adaptability, customer engagement, operational excellence, financial health, team strength, and industry networking. By continuously refining these elements, you can ensure that your business not only sustains its current success but also remains poised for perpetual growth.

Maintaining operational excellence is essential for sustaining success. Efficient operations minimize costs, reduce downtime, and ensure a consistent customer experience. Implementing a preventive maintenance schedule that includes regular inspections and servicing of your vending machines can prevent breakdowns and extend the lifespan of your equipment. Providing your team with detailed troubleshooting guides for common issues can ensure quick resolution of problems and minimize downtime. Building strong relationships with suppliers to ensure a steady supply of quality products can help maintain product availability and respond quickly to changes in demand. Using inventory management software to track stock levels in real-time can help optimize restocking schedules and prevent stock-outs or overstocking. Analyzing sales data to forecast demand and adjust inventory levels accordingly can reduce waste and improve profitability. Implementing automated restocking systems that trigger orders based on predefined inventory thresholds can streamline operations and ensure product availability.

One of the cornerstones of sustained success is the ability to adapt to changing market conditions and consumer preferences. The vending machine industry is dynamic, with new technologies, products, and consumer behaviors emerging regularly. To stay ahead, you must embrace innovation and be willing to adapt your strategies accordingly. Investing in smart vending machines that offer cashless payments, remote monitoring, and real-time inventory tracking can enhance operational efficiency and customer convenience. Utilizing data analytics to gain insights into customer preferences and buying patterns can help optimize product selection, pricing, and restocking schedules. Developing a mobile app that allows customers to locate your vending machines, check product availability, and make purchases can enhance the customer experience and drive more sales. Staying abreast of health trends and dietary preferences by offering healthy snacks, gluten-free options, and other specialty products can attract health-conscious consumers and broaden your customer base. Rotating your product offerings to include seasonal items can boost sales and keep your offerings fresh and exciting. Introducing limited edition products or exclusive collaborations with local brands can create a sense of urgency and encourage repeat purchases.

Adapting to a Changing Marketplace

Staying Ahead of Evolving Consumer Preferences

Adapting to changing consumer demands requires a proactive approach, integrating healthier options, catering to dietary restrictions, and leveraging social media listening to identify new product opportunities. Here's how to effectively navigate these shifts and keep your vending machines relevant and appealing.

Offering Healthier Options

Today's consumers are increasingly health-conscious, seeking nutritious and wholesome snack and beverage choices. Integrating healthier options into your vending machines can attract a broader customer base and meet the demands of this growing market segment.

Healthy Snacks and Beverages: Stock items such as granola bars, dried fruits, nuts, yogurt, and low-sugar drinks. These products cater to health-conscious individuals looking for convenient yet nutritious options.

Transparency in Ingredients: Provide clear information about the nutritional content and ingredients of your products. Transparency builds trust and helps customers make informed choices, especially those who are health-focused.

Rotating Seasonal Items: Introduce seasonal healthy products to keep your offerings fresh and exciting. Seasonal items can include locally sourced fruits in summer or wholesome soups in winter, aligning with consumer preferences throughout the year.

Catering to Dietary Restrictions

Addressing dietary restrictions is essential for inclusivity and customer satisfaction. By offering products that cater to various dietary needs, you can expand your customer base and enhance the overall appeal of your vending machines.

Gluten-Free and Vegan Options: Stock gluten-free snacks and vegan products to cater to those with specific dietary requirements. Products like gluten-free crackers, vegan protein bars, and plant-based beverages can attract customers with these needs.

Allergen-Friendly Choices: Include items that are free from common allergens such as nuts, dairy, and soy. Clearly label these products to ensure customers can easily identify safe options.

Specialty Diets: Consider offering products suitable for specialty diets such as keto, paleo, or low-carb. These options can appeal to customers following specific dietary regimens and differentiate your vending machines from competitors.

Utilizing Social Media Listening

Social media listening involves monitoring social media platforms for mentions of your brand, products, and industry trends. This strategy provides valuable insights into consumer preferences and emerging trends, allowing you to adapt quickly and effectively.

Identifying Trends: Use social media listening tools to track trending topics and hashtags related to snacks, beverages, and health foods. This can help you identify new product opportunities and understand what consumers are currently interested in.

Customer Feedback: Monitor customer reviews and comments on social media to gather direct feedback on your products. Positive feedback can highlight popular items, while negative comments can pinpoint areas for improvement.

Engaging With Consumers: Actively engage with your audience on social media by responding to comments, conducting polls, and asking for product suggestions. This interaction fosters a sense of community and makes customers feel valued and heard.

Competitor Analysis: Analyze the social media activity of your competitors to identify successful strategies and product offerings. Understanding what works for others in the industry can inspire new ideas and improvements for your own business.

Implementing Changes Based on Insights

The data and insights gathered from social media listening should inform your product selection and marketing strategies. Regularly update your inventory to reflect the latest trends and preferences, ensuring your vending machines remain relevant and appealing.

Collaborating with Suppliers: Work closely with your suppliers to source new and trending products. Strong supplier relationships can facilitate quicker adaptation to market changes and ensure a steady supply of popular items.

Marketing New Products: Promote new and trendy products through targeted marketing campaigns. Use social media, in-machine displays, and email newsletters to inform customers about your latest offerings and encourage them to try new items.

Future-Proofing Your Business

Incorporating Self-Service Kiosks

Self-service kiosks represent the next evolution in vending, offering a versatile platform for product delivery and customer interaction. These kiosks can significantly enhance the customer experience and operational efficiency.

Versatility and Convenience: Self-service kiosks can offer a wider range of products compared to traditional vending machines, from snacks and beverages to electronics and personal care items. The digital interface allows for easy browsing, selection, and payment, enhancing the overall convenience for the customer.

Data Collection and Personalization: Self-service kiosks can collect valuable data on customer preferences and purchasing behavior. This data can be used to tailor product offerings, create personalized promotions, and improve inventory management. The ability to gather and analyze customer data in real-time enables you to make informed decisions that drive sales and customer satisfaction.

Reducing Operational Costs: While the initial investment in self-service kiosks may be higher, they can reduce long-term operational costs through automation and reduced need for staff intervention. This efficiency can result in significant savings and higher profit margins over time.

Implementing Data-Driven Marketing Campaigns

Data-driven marketing is a powerful tool for engaging customers and driving sales. By leveraging data analytics, you can create targeted marketing campaigns that resonate with your audience and achieve better results.

Understanding Customer Behavior: Utilize data analytics to gain insights into customer behavior, such as purchasing patterns, peak buying times, and product preferences. This information allows you to create marketing campaigns that are highly relevant and personalized.

Targeted Promotions: Based on the data collected, design targeted promotions that cater to specific customer segments. For example, if data shows that certain products are popular among young adults, create promotions specifically aimed at that demographic. Tailored promotions are more likely to capture the attention of customers and encourage repeat purchases.

Real-Time Campaign Adjustments: Data-driven marketing allows for real-time monitoring and adjustments. Track the performance of your campaigns and make necessary changes to optimize results. This agility ensures that your marketing efforts remain effective and aligned with current trends.

Leveraging Social Media: Integrate your data-driven marketing campaigns with social media platforms to reach a wider audience. Use targeted ads and engage with customers through social media channels to build brand awareness and loyalty. Social media listening tools can also provide additional insights into customer preferences and emerging trends.

Future Trends and Adaptation

Staying at the forefront of the vending industry requires continuous adaptation to future trends. Keep an eye on emerging technologies and consumer behaviors to ensure your business remains competitive.

Emerging Technologies: Be open to adopting new technologies that can enhance your operations and customer experience. This could include advancements in artificial intelligence, machine learning, and the Internet of Things (IoT), which can provide deeper insights and more efficient management of your vending machines.

Sustainability Practices: As consumers become more environmentally conscious, incorporating sustainable practices into your business can set you apart from competitors. Use energy-efficient machines, offer eco-friendly products, and implement recycling programs to appeal to eco-conscious customers.

Future-proofing your vending machine business involves a multifaceted approach that embraces cashless technology, incorporates self-service kiosks, and leverages data-driven marketing campaigns. By staying adaptable and open to new technologies and trends, you can ensure your business remains competitive and continues to grow. These strategies not only meet current consumer demands but also position your business to thrive in the evolving market landscape.

Building a Vending Machine Legacy

Building a lasting legacy in the vending machine business involves more than just meeting revenue targets; it requires cultivating strong brand loyalty and fostering deep customer relationships. Social media is a powerful tool for achieving these goals. By leveraging social media platforms effectively, you can engage with your customers, enhance their experience, and encourage repeat business. Here's how to utilize social media to build a strong and loyal customer base.

Understanding the Power of Social Media Connection

Creating Engaging Content

The first step in leveraging social media is to create engaging content that captures the interest of your audience. This content should be relevant, informative, and entertaining. Here are some types of content that can help build brand loyalty:

Product Highlights: Regularly post about the products available in your vending machines. Use high-quality images and videos to showcase new and popular items. Highlight unique selling points, such as healthy options, eco-friendly packaging, or locally sourced products.

Behind-the-Scenes Glimpses: Share behind-the-scenes content that gives customers a peek into the operations of your vending machine business. This could include videos of how machines are stocked, maintenance routines, or interviews with your staff.

Such content humanizes your brand and builds a connection with your audience.

Customer Stories: Feature stories and testimonials from satisfied customers. Encourage customers to share their experiences and tag your brand in their posts. Sharing user-generated content not only builds trust but also creates a sense of community.

Promotions and Special Offers: Use social media to announce promotions, discounts, and special offers. Create eye-catching graphics and share them across your platforms to drive traffic to your vending machines. Limited-time offers can create urgency and encourage immediate action.

Interactive Content: Engage your audience with interactive content like polls, quizzes, and contests. Ask for their opinions on new products, favorite snacks, or potential new locations. Interactive content boosts engagement and makes customers feel valued.

Building a Community

Building a loyal customer base requires creating a sense of community around your brand. Social media is ideal for fostering this sense of belonging.

Engage Regularly: Consistently interact with your audience by responding to comments, answering questions, and acknowledging feedback. Show appreciation for positive comments and address any concerns promptly and professionally.

Host Events and Meetups: Organize events or meetups where customers can interact with your brand in person. This could be a launch event for a new vending machine location or a tasting event for new products. Promote these events on social media to generate excitement.

Create Groups and Forums: Establish dedicated groups or forums on platforms like Facebook or LinkedIn where customers can share their experiences, ask questions, and connect with others. Actively participate in these groups to foster a supportive and engaged community.

Collaborate With Influencers

Partnering with social media influencers can significantly boost your brand's visibility and credibility. Influencers have established followings that trust their recommendations. Here's how to collaborate with influencers:

Identify Relevant Influencers: Look for influencers whose audience aligns with your target market. They could be food bloggers, health and wellness advocates, or local personalities.

Create Authentic Partnerships: Work with influencers to create authentic content that showcases your products. This could include product reviews, unboxing videos, or sponsored posts. Ensure that the content aligns with your brand's values and messaging.

Monitor and Measure Impact: Track the performance of influencer collaborations to measure their impact on brand awareness and sales. Use metrics like engagement rates, follower growth, and sales conversions to evaluate success.

Utilizing Social Media Analytics

To maximize the effectiveness of your social media efforts, use analytics tools to track performance and gain insights into your audience's behavior. Social media platforms offer built-in analytics that provide valuable data on post engagement, audience demographics, and trends.

Analyze Engagement: Monitor which types of content generate the most engagement. Use this information to refine your content strategy and focus on what resonates with your audience.

Track Growth: Keep an eye on follower growth and engagement metrics to understand the impact of your social media activities. Regularly review these metrics to identify areas for improvement.

Adjust Strategies: Use insights from social media analytics to adjust your strategies. For example, if certain types of posts consistently perform well, create more of that content. If engagement drops, experiment with new formats or topics.

Cultivating brand loyalty through social media involves creating engaging content, building a community, collaborating with influencers, and utilizing analytics to refine your approach. By actively engaging with your audience and providing value through your social media presence, you can build strong customer relationships and encourage repeat business. This approach not only enhances your brand's reputation but also ensures long-term success and sustainability in the competitive vending machine industry. Embrace the power of social media to create a loyal customer base and leave a lasting legacy in the vending world.

The Power of Community Engagement

Engaging with your community through charitable initiatives is a powerful way to build a positive brand image and foster customer loyalty. When customers see a business actively contributing to their community, it strengthens their emotional connection to the brand and enhances their overall perception. Here's how to effectively give back to the community and build a lasting, positive brand image.

Supporting Local Charities

Partnering with local charities can have a significant impact. Collaborate with organizations that align with your brand's values and mission. For example, if your vending machines offer healthy snacks, you might partner with health and wellness charities. Donations can take various forms, such as a portion of your sales, providing free products for charity events, or sponsoring community programs.

Organizing fundraisers is another effective strategy. Host events or online campaigns to support causes that matter to your community. You can set up donation boxes at your vending machines or promote charity drives through your social media channels. Fundraising not only supports important causes but also engages your customers and encourages them to participate.

Product Donations

Product donations can make a big difference in your community. Donate surplus or near-expiry products to local shelters, food banks, and community centers. This ensures that your products are used effectively and helps those in need. Promote these donations on social media to highlight your commitment to the community, which can enhance your brand's image and inspire others to contribute.

Employee Involvement

Encourage your employees to participate in community service projects. Offer paid time off for volunteering and organize team volunteer days. Employee involvement in charitable activities fosters a sense of pride and loyalty within your workforce. It also demonstrates your company's dedication to social responsibility, which can improve your brand's reputation.

Transparent Communication

Communicate your community engagement efforts clearly and regularly. Use your website, social media, and email newsletters to share stories and updates about your charitable initiatives. Transparency builds trust and shows your commitment to making a positive impact. Highlight success stories and testimonials from the beneficiaries of your efforts to illustrate the tangible impact of your initiatives.

Engaging With the Community

Engage actively with your community both online and offline. Respond to comments and messages on social media, attend local events, and participate in community discussions. Showing that you're accessible and genuinely interested in your community's well-being enhances your brand's reputation.

Sustainability Practices

Integrate sustainable practices into your business operations. Use eco-friendly products, reduce waste, and support environmental initiatives. Promoting your sustainability efforts aligns with the values of environmentally conscious consumers and reinforces a positive brand image.

Consistency and Feedback

Consistency in community engagement is crucial. Regularly support local initiatives and maintain ongoing partnerships with charities and community organizations. Consistent involvement shows that your commitment is genuine and long-term. Solicit feedback from the community about your engagement efforts, listen to their suggestions, and adapt your strategies to better meet their needs.

Celebrating Milestones

Celebrate and share milestones in your community engagement journey. Whether it's reaching a fundraising goal, completing a volunteer project, or launching a new partnership, celebrating these achievements with your community fosters a sense of shared success.

Impact on Business Success

Community engagement drives business success by enhancing customer loyalty, increasing brand awareness, and improving employee satisfaction. Customers are more likely to support and remain loyal to brands that demonstrate social responsibility. Charitable initiatives and community involvement boost your brand's visibility through positive media coverage and social media shares. Employees take pride in working for a socially responsible company, improving morale, job satisfaction, and retention.

Building a Vending Machine Empire

Franchising Your Business Model

Franchising offers a proven pathway for rapid expansion. By allowing others to replicate your successful business model, you can grow your brand and increase your market footprint with minimal capital investment.

Benefits of Franchising: Franchising enables you to scale your business quickly without the need for significant upfront capital. Franchisees invest their own money to open new locations, reducing your financial risk. Additionally, franchisees often bring local market knowledge and a vested interest in the success of their franchise, driving overall business growth.

Developing a Franchise Model: To franchise your vending machine business, start by developing a comprehensive franchise model. This includes creating detailed operational guidelines, training programs, and support systems to ensure consistency across all franchise locations. Your franchise package should cover all aspects of running the business, from machine placement and product selection to marketing and maintenance.

Legal Considerations: Franchising involves complex legal considerations. You'll need to prepare a Franchise Disclosure Document (FDD) that outlines all the terms and conditions of the franchise agreement. It's essential to work with a legal expert to ensure compliance with federal and state regulations.

Selecting Franchisees: Choose franchisees carefully to maintain your brand's integrity. Look for individuals with a strong business background, financial stability, and a passion for the vending industry. Providing robust support and training will help franchisees succeed and uphold your brand's reputation.

Expanding Into Other Vending Machine-Related Ventures

Diversifying your business by exploring related ventures can open new revenue streams and enhance your market position. Here are some potential expansion opportunities:

Micro Markets: Micro markets are unattended, self-service retail spaces that offer a variety of products, including fresh food, beverages, and snacks. They are typically set up in office buildings, gyms, and other high-traffic areas. Micro markets provide a more extensive product selection than traditional vending machines, catering to customers seeking convenience and variety. Setting up micro markets can be a profitable extension of your vending business.

Smart Vending Machines: Invest in smart vending machines equipped with advanced technology like touchscreens, artificial intelligence, and IoT connectivity. These machines can offer personalized product recommendations, accept multiple payment methods, and provide real-time inventory tracking. Smart vending machines enhance the customer experience and can lead to increased sales and customer loyalty.

Automated Retail: Expand into automated retail by offering a broader range of products beyond snacks and beverages. Automated retail machines can sell electronics, beauty products, apparel, and more. These machines can be placed in airports, shopping malls, and other high-traffic locations, providing convenience and generating substantial revenue.

Healthy Vending: Capitalize on the growing demand for healthy snack options by launching a line of vending machines dedicated to nutritious products. Stock these machines with items like fresh fruits, salads, protein bars, and organic snacks. Partnering with health and wellness organizations can further boost your brand's credibility and attract health-conscious consumers.

Subscription Services: Introduce subscription-based services where customers can sign up to receive regular deliveries of their favorite vending machine products. This model provides a steady revenue stream and enhances customer loyalty. Offer personalized subscription plans based on customer preferences and consumption patterns.

Corporate Partnerships: Establish partnerships with corporations to place your vending machines in their offices and facilities. Corporate partnerships can provide a stable and lucrative customer base. Offer customized solutions, such as machines stocked with employee favorites or products that align with corporate wellness programs.

International Expansion: Consider expanding your vending machine business internationally. Research potential markets to understand local consumer preferences, regulatory requirements, and competition. International expansion can significantly boost your brand's global presence and revenue.

Marketing and Branding for Expansion

Effective marketing and branding are crucial for successfully expanding your vending machine empire. Develop a strong brand identity that resonates with your target audience. Use social media, content marketing, and PR campaigns to build brand awareness and attract potential franchisees or partners.

Customer Engagement: Continuously engage with your customers through various channels to gather feedback and understand their needs. Use this information to refine your product offerings and improve customer satisfaction.

Innovative Promotions: Implement innovative marketing promotions to attract new customers and retain existing ones. Offer loyalty programs, discounts, and limited-time offers to drive sales and enhance brand loyalty.

Building a vending machine empire through franchising or expanding into related ventures offers significant growth opportunities. Franchising allows for rapid scaling with minimal capital investment, while diversification into areas like micro markets, smart vending machines, and healthy vending can open new revenue streams. By developing a robust franchise model, exploring innovative ventures, and implementing effective marketing strategies, you can create a thriving, multifaceted vending machine business. Embrace these opportunities to expand your market presence, increase profitability, and build a lasting legacy in the vending industry.

Chapter 12
Beyond the Equation: The Vending Machine Journey

The true essence of building a successful business lies not only in the numbers but also in the impact you create, the lives you touch, and the personal growth you experience along the way.

Running a vending machine business can be incredibly rewarding on many levels. It's not just about the profit margins or hitting the $500,000 revenue mark. It's about finding a sense of purpose and joy in what you do. Personal fulfillment comes from knowing that your efforts are making a positive impact on your customers, your community, and your own life.

While financial success is a significant aspect of any business, finding personal meaning and satisfaction in your work is equally important. Consider the satisfaction of providing convenient, healthy snacks to people on the go, or the joy of seeing a child's face light up when they get their favorite treat from your machine. These moments of connection and service can bring immense personal gratification.

Beyond the immediate customer interactions, think about the broader impact your business can have. By choosing to stock environmentally friendly products, you contribute to a more sustainable future. By partnering with local charities, you support your community and make a tangible difference in people's lives. These actions add layers of fulfillment that transcend financial achievements.

Entrepreneurship is more than a career path; it's a way of life. The journey of building a successful vending machine business is filled with challenges and triumphs that shape you as an individual. There's a unique sense of accomplishment that comes from turning an idea into a thriving business. Every machine you install, every problem you solve, and every customer you serve contributes to your growth as an entrepreneur.

The entrepreneurial spirit is characterized by resilience, creativity, and a relentless pursuit of excellence. It's about finding joy in the journey, not just the destination. The skills you develop, the relationships you build, and the experiences you gain are invaluable. They not only contribute to your business success but also enrich your personal life.

The Value of Personal Fulfillment

More Than Just Money

In the fast-paced world of business, it's easy to get caught up in the numbers—profits, revenues, margins, and growth rates. However, true success in the vending machine business, as in any venture, lies beyond mere financial achievements. It's about finding personal meaning and satisfaction in what you do. This deeper sense of fulfillment can drive you, sustain you through challenges, and provide a lasting sense of accomplishment that money alone cannot offer. Here's why finding personal meaning in your business is crucial and how you can achieve it.

The Limitations of Financial Success

While financial success is a significant motivator and a necessary component of any business, it has its limitations. Profits can buy comfort and security, but they don't necessarily lead to happiness or fulfillment. Many successful entrepreneurs find that after reaching their financial goals, there remains a void, a search for something more meaningful.

Money can provide the means to enjoy life's pleasures, but it's not the ultimate source of happiness. Beyond a certain point, increasing wealth doesn't proportionately increase personal satisfaction. This is where the importance of personal fulfillment comes into play. It's about finding joy and purpose in your daily activities and knowing that your work has a positive impact.

Creating Impact Beyond Profits

One way to find personal meaning in your business is by focusing on the impact you create. For instance, by stocking your vending machines with healthy snack options, you contribute to the well-being of your customers. Promoting sustainable practices by using eco-friendly packaging and reducing waste can also be deeply satisfying. These actions not only benefit your business but also contribute positively to society and the environment.

Supporting local suppliers and small businesses by including their products in your vending machines can also create a sense of fulfillment. By doing so, you help other entrepreneurs succeed and foster a sense of community. The ripple effect of your business decisions can lead to widespread positive impacts, reinforcing the value of your work.

Building Relationships and Community

The relationships you build with customers, employees, suppliers, and the community play a significant role in finding personal fulfillment. Knowing that your business provides convenience and enjoyment to people's lives can be incredibly rewarding. Engaging with customers and receiving their feedback gives you a sense of connection and purpose.

Your employees also contribute to your sense of fulfillment. Creating a supportive and positive work environment where your team feels valued and motivated can bring immense satisfaction. Their growth and success within your company reflect your effectiveness as a leader and mentor.

Involvement in community initiatives and charitable activities can further enhance your sense of purpose. Sponsoring local events, donating to charities, or participating in community service projects not only strengthens your brand but also enriches your life. These actions remind you that your business can be a force for good.

Personal Growth and Achievement

Running a successful vending machine business is a journey of personal growth and achievement. Overcoming challenges, solving problems, and seeing your efforts come to fruition provides a deep sense of accomplishment. Each milestone reached, whether it's expanding to a new location, launching a new product line, or hitting a sales target, is a testament to your hard work and determination.

The entrepreneurial journey fosters resilience, creativity, and adaptability. These skills are valuable not only in business but in all areas of life. Personal growth often leads to a greater understanding of oneself and one's values, which in turn enhances personal fulfillment.

Balancing Work and Life

Personal fulfillment also comes from achieving a balance between work and personal life. While dedication to your business is crucial, it's equally important to make time for family, friends, hobbies, and relaxation. A well-rounded life where you can pursue your passions and spend time with loved ones contributes significantly to overall happiness.

Work-life balance prevents burnout and keeps you motivated. It allows you to return to your business with renewed energy and creativity. Ensuring that your business operations can run smoothly even in your absence is a mark of successful entrepreneurship and personal well-being.

Leaving a Legacy

Ultimately, personal fulfillment in business is about the legacy you leave behind. It's about building something that outlasts you and continues to have a positive impact. Whether it's a brand known for quality and integrity, a community enriched by your contributions, or employees who have grown and succeeded because of your leadership, your legacy is a powerful source of fulfillment.

Your business can be more than just a means to make money; it can be a vehicle for positive change, personal growth, and lasting impact. By focusing on these aspects, you find deeper meaning and satisfaction in your work, making your entrepreneurial journey truly rewarding.

The Entrepreneurial Spirit

The entrepreneurial journey is one of the most challenging yet rewarding paths one can take. It involves the relentless pursuit of turning a vision into reality, facing obstacles head-on, and finding joy in the process of building something meaningful. The vending machine business, like any entrepreneurial endeavor, offers unique opportunities to experience a profound sense of accomplishment, create joy in your work, and make a lasting impact on your customers and community.

The Sense of Accomplishment

The sense of accomplishment derived from building a successful business is unparalleled. Each milestone, whether it's your first vending machine installation, reaching a significant sales target, or expanding to new locations, serves as a testament to your hard work, resilience, and ingenuity.

Achieving these milestones is not just about the results but also about the journey. Overcoming challenges, solving problems, and continually improving your operations all contribute to a deep sense of fulfillment. Each success story is a reflection of your dedication and an affirmation that your efforts are making a difference.

Moreover, as your business grows, the sense of accomplishment expands beyond personal achievements. Seeing your team succeed, your customers satisfied, and your community benefiting from your services brings an added layer of gratification. This cumulative sense of achievement motivates you to set higher goals and continue striving for excellence.

The Joy of Building a Successful Business

Building a successful vending machine business is a source of immense joy. This joy comes from the creative process, the daily operations, and the relationships you build along the way. There's a unique pleasure in creating a business from scratch, seeing your ideas come to life, and watching your vision take shape.

One of the key joys of entrepreneurship is the freedom it offers. As a business owner, you have the autonomy to make decisions, innovate, and steer your business in the direction you believe in. This freedom fosters a sense of ownership and responsibility that is deeply satisfying.

The daily interactions with customers, employees, and partners also bring joy. Engaging with your customers, understanding their needs, and seeing their satisfaction with your products provide a continuous source of motivation. Building a strong, supportive team and fostering a positive work environment enhances your daily experience and contributes to overall happiness.

Furthermore, the joy of entrepreneurship often lies in the small victories. Each successful transaction, positive customer feedback, and operational improvement adds to the daily joys of running your business. These moments remind you why you embarked on this journey and reinforce your passion for your work.

The Impact on Customers and Community

One of the most rewarding aspects of entrepreneurship is the impact you can create on your customers and community. Through your vending machine business, you have the opportunity to provide convenience, quality products, and exceptional service to your customers.

Your vending machines can cater to various needs, whether it's providing a quick snack for a busy professional, a healthy option for a health-conscious individual, or a refreshing drink on a hot day. By carefully selecting your product offerings, you can meet diverse preferences and enhance the customer experience.

Beyond serving individual customers, your business can make a broader impact on the community. Supporting local suppliers and small businesses by including their products in your vending machines strengthens the local economy. Engaging in community events, sponsoring local initiatives, and participating in charitable activities further embeds your business within the community fabric.

Your business can also promote positive values. For example, by offering sustainable and eco-friendly products, you encourage environmentally conscious behavior among your customers. By focusing on health and wellness, you contribute to the overall well-being of the community.

Creating a Legacy

The impact of your entrepreneurial efforts extends beyond the present. By building a reputable and successful business, you create a legacy that can influence future generations. Your business can become a pillar in the community, known for its quality, integrity, and positive contributions.

Mentoring aspiring entrepreneurs, sharing your experiences, and supporting local education initiatives can inspire others to pursue their entrepreneurial dreams. Your journey and success can serve as a beacon of possibility, demonstrating that with dedication, innovation, and resilience, great achievements are possible.

The Path to Continuous Learning

Embracing Continuous Learning:

The Dynamic Nature of the Vending Machine Industry

The vending machine industry, like many others, is subject to rapid changes driven by technological advancements, shifting consumer preferences, and evolving market dynamics. Staying informed about these changes is vital to keep your business relevant and competitive.

Technological Advancements: Technology plays a significant role in the vending machine industry. Innovations such as cashless payment systems, remote monitoring, smart vending machines, and data analytics are transforming how vending businesses operate. Keeping abreast of these advancements enables you to integrate the latest technology into your operations, enhancing efficiency, customer experience, and profitability.

Consumer Preferences: Consumer tastes and preferences are constantly changing. Today's consumers are more health-conscious, environmentally aware, and technologically savvy than ever before. Understanding these trends allows you to tailor your product offerings and marketing strategies to meet current demands, ensuring customer satisfaction and loyalty.

Market Dynamics: Economic shifts, regulatory changes, and competitive pressures all impact the vending machine industry. Staying updated on market dynamics helps you anticipate challenges, seize opportunities, and make informed decisions that drive business growth.

Sources of Continuous Learning

To stay updated, leverage a variety of sources for continuous learning. Here are some key resources:

Industry Conferences and Trade Shows: Attending industry conferences and trade shows is an excellent way to learn about the latest trends, products, and technologies. These events provide opportunities to network with other professionals, exchange ideas, and gain insights from industry leaders. Participating in workshops and seminars at these events can enhance your knowledge and skills.

Industry Publications and Websites: Subscribing to industry-specific magazines, journals, and websites keeps you informed about the latest developments. Regularly reading articles, case studies, and reports can provide valuable insights into best practices, emerging technologies, and market trends.

Online Courses and Webinars: Many platforms offer online courses and webinars tailored to the vending machine industry.

These resources allow you to learn at your own pace and stay updated on specific topics such as inventory management, customer engagement, and technology integration. Webinars often feature experts who share their knowledge and experiences, providing practical tips and strategies.

Professional Associations: Joining professional associations related to the vending machine industry can be highly beneficial. These organizations often provide members with access to exclusive resources, training programs, and networking events. Being part of a professional community allows you to stay connected with peers and industry leaders.

Peer Networking: Building relationships with other vending machine business owners can facilitate knowledge sharing and mutual support. Networking groups, forums, and social media communities provide platforms to discuss challenges, share solutions, and learn from each other's experiences.

Implementing Continuous Learning in Your Business

Integrating continuous learning into your business strategy involves a proactive approach. Here's how to implement it effectively:

Create a Learning Culture: Foster a culture of learning within your organization. Encourage your team to stay curious, seek out new information, and share their knowledge. Provide opportunities for professional development through training programs, workshops, and courses. Recognize and reward employees who actively engage in learning and apply their knowledge to improve the business.

Set Learning Goals: Establish specific learning goals for yourself and your team. These goals should align with your business objectives and address areas where you need to enhance your skills or knowledge. Regularly review and adjust these goals to ensure continuous improvement.

Schedule Regular Learning Activities: Allocate time for learning activities in your business schedule. This could include attending industry events, participating in online courses, or dedicating time to read industry publications. Making learning a regular part of your routine ensures that it remains a priority.

Leverage Technology: Use technology to facilitate learning. Online platforms, webinars, and virtual conferences make it easier to access information and stay updated. Implement digital tools for knowledge management, allowing your team to share resources and collaborate on learning initiatives.

Monitor Industry Trends: Keep a close eye on industry trends and developments. Subscribe to newsletters, set up news alerts, and follow industry influencers on social media. Regularly reviewing this information helps you stay informed and anticipate changes that could impact your business.

Apply What You Learn: Continuous learning is most effective when applied practically. Encourage your team to implement new knowledge and skills in their daily tasks. Experiment with new strategies, technologies, and approaches to see what works best for your business. Learning through application reinforces knowledge and drives innovation.

Evaluate and Adjust: Periodically evaluate the effectiveness of your learning initiatives. Assess how well you and your team are staying updated and how the new knowledge is impacting your business. Use this evaluation to adjust your learning strategies and ensure they continue to meet your needs.

Building a Network of Vending Machine Professionals

The value of a strong professional network cannot be overstated. Building and maintaining connections with other vending machine business owners offers numerous benefits, from knowledge sharing and support to collaboration opportunities and industry insights. Here's how and why you should focus on building a network of vending machine professionals.

Networking provides a platform for exchanging ideas, experiences, and best practices. It allows you to learn from the successes and failures of others, gain new perspectives, and stay informed about industry trends. A robust network can also offer emotional support, helping you navigate the challenges and uncertainties of running a business.

Knowledge Sharing

One of the primary benefits of networking is the opportunity to share knowledge. Engaging with other business owners allows you to exchange valuable information about various aspects of the vending machine industry, including:

Operational Best Practices: Learn how other business owners manage their operations, from inventory control and machine maintenance to route optimization and customer service. Sharing tips and strategies can help you improve efficiency and reduce costs.

Technological Advancements: Stay updated on the latest technological innovations in the vending industry. Whether it's new payment systems, remote monitoring tools, or smart vending machines, knowledge sharing ensures you are aware of the latest advancements and can adopt them to stay competitive.

Market Trends: Discussing market trends with peers helps you understand changing consumer preferences and emerging opportunities. This knowledge enables you to adapt your product offerings and marketing strategies to meet current demands.

Regulatory Updates: Keep informed about regulatory changes that may impact your business. Networking provides a channel for discussing compliance issues and sharing insights on navigating new regulations.

Support and Collaboration

Running a vending machine business can be isolating, especially for solo entrepreneurs. Building a network of peers provides a support system where you can share challenges, seek advice, and offer encouragement. This emotional and professional support is invaluable for maintaining motivation and resilience.

Problem Solving: When you encounter challenges, such as declining sales or operational issues, your network can provide practical solutions based on their experiences. Collaborating with others to brainstorm and troubleshoot can lead to innovative solutions that you might not have considered on your own.

Collaboration Opportunities: Networking can open doors to collaboration opportunities that benefit all parties involved. Joint ventures, bulk purchasing agreements, or co-marketing initiatives can enhance your business operations and expand your reach. Collaborating with other vending machine owners allows you to leverage collective resources and expertise.

Industry Events and Associations

Participating in industry events and joining professional associations are effective ways to build and strengthen your network. These platforms provide opportunities for face-to-face interactions, learning, and relationship-building.

Industry Conferences and Trade Shows: Attend vending machine industry conferences and trade shows to meet other business owners, vendors, and industry experts. These events offer a wealth of information through seminars, workshops, and presentations. They also provide a space to discuss trends, challenges, and opportunities with your peers.

Professional Associations: Join industry-specific professional associations such as the National Automatic Merchandising Association (NAMA) or other local vending associations. Membership in these organizations often includes access to exclusive resources, training programs, and networking events. Being part of a professional community enhances your credibility and keeps you connected with industry developments.

Online Communities and Social Media

In addition to in-person events, online communities and social media platforms offer valuable networking opportunities. Engaging in online forums, discussion groups, and social media pages dedicated to the vending machine industry can expand your network and provide continuous learning.

Online Forums: Participate in online forums and discussion groups where vending machine professionals share insights and experiences. Platforms like Reddit, LinkedIn Groups, and specialized industry forums are excellent places to ask questions, share knowledge, and connect with peers.

Social Media Networking: Use social media platforms like LinkedIn, Twitter, and Facebook to follow industry leaders, join relevant groups, and participate in discussions. Social media allows you to stay updated on industry news, trends, and events, and provides a space to engage with a broader network of professionals.

Building Strong Relationships

Networking is more than just making connections; it's about

building strong, meaningful relationships. Here are some tips for fostering genuine relationships within your professional network:

Be Authentic: Approach networking with authenticity and a genuine interest in others. Focus on building trust and rapport rather than just seeking immediate benefits.

Offer Value: Networking is a two-way street. Be willing to share your knowledge, experiences, and resources. Offering value to your connections strengthens relationships and encourages reciprocity.

Stay in Touch: Maintain regular contact with your network. Follow up after events, send occasional updates, and check in to see how your connections are doing. Consistent communication keeps relationships strong and ensures you remain top of mind.

Be Supportive: Offer support and encouragement to your peers. Celebrate their successes, provide assistance during challenges, and be a reliable resource. Building a supportive network creates a positive, collaborative environment where everyone benefits.

The Never-Ending Vending Machine

Like the rhythmic hum of a well-oiled vending machine, the pursuit of success, growth, and fulfillment is a continuous cycle —a testament to resilience, innovation, and passion.

The Journey Begins Anew

Every dawn brings a new opportunity to innovate, to serve, and to grow. The vending machine, a symbol of convenience and accessibility, mirrors the ceaseless rhythm of an entrepreneur's journey. Each time you stock a machine, analyze data, or interact with a customer, you contribute to an ongoing story of dedication and progress. The entrepreneurial spirit thrives on this perpetual motion, finding joy in both the routine and the unexpected.

Embracing Change

Change is the only constant, and in the vending machine industry, adaptability is your greatest ally. The world evolves—new technologies emerge, consumer preferences shift, and markets fluctuate. Embracing these changes with open arms and a curious mind transforms challenges into opportunities. Each innovation, from cashless payment systems to sustainable products, represents a step forward, a chance to refine your business and better serve your customers.

A Community of Dreamers

You are not alone in this journey. Look around, and you'll find a community of dreamers, doers, and visionaries. Fellow vending machine operators, suppliers, and customers—each one contributes to the tapestry of your business. By building strong connections and fostering a supportive network, you create a foundation that withstands the test of time. Collaboration and mutual support amplify your strengths and provide solace during the inevitable trials.

The Human Touch

At its core, the vending machine business is deeply human. Each transaction is a small act of trust, a moment of connection between you and your customer. The smile of a satisfied patron, the repeat business of a loyal client—these are the true rewards that go beyond monetary gains. Your machines serve more than snacks and drinks; they deliver moments of delight, convenience, and satisfaction.

The Legacy of Innovation

Innovation is the heart of enduring success. Just as vending machines have evolved from simple coin-operated devices to sophisticated, smart machines, your business must continually adapt and innovate. This legacy of innovation is not just about staying relevant but about pushing boundaries and setting new standards. It's about dreaming bigger and striving for excellence in every aspect of your business.

Resilience and Tenacity

The entrepreneurial journey is fraught with challenges. Machines break down, sales fluctuate, competition intensifies. Yet, it is your resilience and tenacity that define your path. Each setback is a lesson, each challenge an opportunity to grow stronger. The ability to persevere, to find solutions, and to keep moving forward is the hallmark of a true entrepreneur.

Personal Fulfillment

Beyond the numbers and the operations, there lies personal fulfillment. The sense of accomplishment when you see your business thrive, the joy in knowing that you've created something valuable, and the pride in contributing positively to your community—these are the intangible rewards that fuel your journey. Your work is not just a means to an end; it is a source of personal meaning and satisfaction.

Continuous Learning

The quest for knowledge never ends. Staying informed about industry trends, best practices, and emerging technologies is crucial. Embrace every opportunity to learn, to grow, and to improve. Continuous learning keeps your mind sharp, your strategies relevant, and your business thriving. It ensures that you are always prepared to meet the future, no matter what it holds.

Leaving a Legacy

As you look back on your journey, consider the legacy you wish to leave. It's not just about the profits or the number of machines you own. It's about the impact you've made, the lives you've touched, and the values you've upheld. Your legacy is built on integrity, innovation, and the relentless pursuit of excellence. It's a testament to your dedication and passion, inspiring future generations of entrepreneurs.

A Never-Ending Story

The story of your vending machine business is a never-ending one. Each day brings new opportunities, new challenges, and new triumphs. It's a story written not just in profits and losses but in the moments of connection, the acts of service, and the relentless drive to make a difference. It's a story of resilience, of growth, and of endless possibilities.

As you turn the last page of this book, remember that the journey is far from over. The never-ending vending machine symbolizes the continuous cycle of innovation, service, and personal fulfillment. Embrace this journey with an open heart and a curious mind. Let your entrepreneurial spirit guide you, and may your business thrive in ways you've never imagined.

In the hum of the vending machine, in the quiet moments of reflection, and in the bustling days of operation, find your purpose, your joy, and your legacy. The path of an entrepreneur is indeed never-ending, but it is also endlessly rewarding. Here's to your journey, your growth, and your success—today and always.

Thank You for Reading!

I hope this book helped lay out a clear path forward in starting and growing your business. Now it's time for me to ask for a little help from you. Your feedback is incredibly valuable to me and helps other readers discover this book.

If you could take a moment to leave a review on your favorite book platform, it would mean a lot.

Thank you for your support!

Best regards,

David Whitehead

www.ingramcontent.com/pod-product-compliance
Lightning Source LLC
Chambersburg PA
CBHW030502210326
41597CB00013B/758